Vision Collections   No.2 Apostles

Apostles
First Followers
and Their Faith

by David Hulme

Vision Media Publishing
Pasadena, California
2010

PUBLISHED BY VISION MEDIA PUBLISHING
P.O. Box 90607
Pasadena, California 91109-0607

© 2010 by Church of God, an International Community

All rights reserved. No part of this publication may be
reproduced, translated, stored in a retrieval system, or
transmitted in any form or by any means, electronic, mechanical,
photocopying, recording or otherwise, without prior written
permission from the publisher.

Vision Collections are compiled and revised from material
previously published in serial form in the quarterly journal *Vision*
(www.vision.org).

Unless otherwise noted, all scripture quotations are from
THE HOLY BIBLE, ENGLISH STANDARD VERSION®, © 2001 by
Crossway Bibles, a publishing ministry of Good News Publishers.
Used by permission. All rights reserved.

Designed by CDT Design
www.cdt-design.co.uk
Illustrations by Simon Pemberton
www.simonpemberton.com
Printed and bound in the United States of America
by The Castle Press
www.castlepress.com
ISBN 978-0-9822828-1-6

Contents

- v   Foreword
- 1   Introduction
- 5   Chapter One: Acting on Conviction
- 23   Chapter Two: Peter, Paul and Barnabas
- 43   Chapter Three: New Team, New Territory
- 63   Chapter Four: From Ephesus to Jerusalem
- 83   Chapter Five: On to Rome
- 99   Chapter Six: Journey's End
- 111   Chapter Seven: James, Brother of Jesus
- 123   Chapter Eight: Feed My Sheep!
- 141   Chapter Nine: What Kind of People Should You Be?
- 155   Chapter Ten: Son of Thunder
- 167   Chapter Eleven: Apostle of Love
- 189   Chapter Twelve: The End Times
- 229   Epilogue

Foreword

When the first century came to an end, the early New Testament Church was under attack from within and without. At its beginning it had grown quickly in numbers and in spiritual strength, but it was not long before corrupt leaders arose, doctrinal error and dissensions spread, pagan philosophies emerged, persecution increased, and the Church diminished in numbers.

By the first part of the second century, it had all but disappeared in the historical record. According to some scholars, it was as if a great curtain came down on the Church—perhaps as early as the 60s, soon after the death of Paul. John, the last surviving of the original 12 apostles, died around 100. When the curtain began to rise again 20 years later, the church that emerged was very different from the body the apostles had nurtured. How different was that original Church from what developed? The story of the first followers of Jesus Christ has been told and retold countless times. Do we really need to repeat it? Surely all that can be said has been said.

The problem is that much of what has been written has come from authors who have filtered their conclusions through the traditions and teachings of a church farther and farther removed from the earliest believers. In addition, these authors have mostly downplayed the importance of understanding the original doctrine of the Church for today. Few have labored to fully understand the teachings and practice of the first followers in their first-century cultural setting and their deep connection to the Hebrew Scriptures. Thus there is a void in the existing literature that needs to be filled.

Another reason to retell this story is that in recent years the notion has circulated that the writers of the New Testament were more often in opposition to each other than united in belief and practice. Though it is true that like all human beings they had their differences of opinion at times and were often writing to different audiences for varying purposes, each with a unique writing style, nevertheless their core beliefs shine through.

Apostles: First Followers and Their Faith helps establish the truth by viewing the lives of these individuals from a more accurate perspective.

I believe there is something to the adage that each generation has to rediscover the essential truths. It is vitally important to review the historical record and assess what we should learn from it. In the case of the New Testament, its truths have stood the test of time, but only as lived honestly by each succeeding generation. Without faithful continuity of belief *and practice,* its message is adulterated and eventually lost. This conviction compelled me to tell the story of Jesus and His original followers anew.

The task of summarizing within a couple of volumes the core of the New Testament is a daunting one. But, realizing that most of us are interested in biography, it occurred to me that the life histories of its key figures might provide the necessary prism.

First came a series of articles about the life of Christ for *Vision* magazine (now in book form as the companion volume to this, titled *Gospels for the 21st Century*). Then a series about the early Church developed. Five years later we were ready to publish in long form what you now hold.

The major personalities discussed in this book practiced what they had received from Jesus. They lived their beliefs. Some even died for them. What they set down—whether as history, as pastoral care or as prophetic instruction—was delivered by real people practicing their belief in the difficult world of the burgeoning Roman imperial superpower.

This book is the result of four decades of study in which I have tried to remove all preconceived ideas about the early Church and to understand more accurately what they believed, taught and practiced. In a sense, it is an attempt to see behind the "curtain" that descended on the Church early in its history.

Whether you accept my assessment or not, I think you will agree that it is a perspective on the New Testament that you will rarely find.

I hope you enjoy this journey through the tumultuous first century of the Church Jesus founded and gain a fresh perspective on these authors, who really did provide timeless teaching.

David Hulme
July 2010

Apostles
First Followers
and Their Faith

Introduction

"Paul did not become a Christian, since there were no Christians in those times."

Pinchas Lapide

The first-century doctor and Gospel writer Luke wrote not only an account of the life of Jesus but also a sequel, a history of the early Church. It is known as the Acts of the Apostles. Some of these earliest leaders also wrote letters to the growing body of believers. They include Paul, James, Jude, Peter and John. Together with the other three Gospels and Acts, their writings make up the New Testament. These documents inform this examination of the lives of Jesus' early followers and of their teachings, beliefs and practices.[1]

Luke dedicated his two histories to Theophilus, meaning "lover of God." This is either a general term for subsequent followers of Jesus, or it is the name of a specific convert and perhaps the author's benefactor. Luke acknowledged that "eyewitnesses and ministers of the word" had produced similar accounts. But, he says, "it seemed good to me also, having followed all things closely for some time past, to write an orderly account for you . . . that you may have certainty concerning the things you have been taught" (Luke 1:3–4, English Standard Version throughout unless otherwise noted).

At first Luke's sequel apparently had no title but was simply treated as a continuation of his earlier Gospel. The first record of it having a title comes around the middle of the second century, when the Greek word *Praxeis* (Acts) was applied to it. Only later was this expanded to *Praxeis Apostolon* (Acts of the Apostles). The Greeks, whose language was the lingua franca of the Roman world, used *praxeis* to describe the achievements of leading figures.

---

[1] The anonymous letter to the Hebrews was in my estimation very likely authored by Paul. Like his letter to the Romans, it is lengthy and deeply doctrinal. Because both demand more complete treatment than is possible in this narrative, these letters are not dealt with here.

If the book's first title was simply Acts, whose acts were of interest? From the title by which we now know it, you might think the account celebrates only the apostles' achievements. Some have gone as far as to say that the focus is really on the accomplishments of only Peter and Paul. But as we will see, many other individuals mentioned in the account achieved a great deal.

Asking the question "Whose acts?" allows us to focus on the central point that Luke is making—that men and women empowered by God accomplish more than they could ever imagine. In reality, it is God's acts through human beings that are demonstrated. Because it is about people and not primarily a statement of beliefs, Luke's sequel is a rich tapestry of human endeavor in the fascinating multicultural world of the first-century Roman Empire. Here we see belief in action. Luke speaks about the followers of Jesus as people who practice "the Way." They are not known as "Christians" but as followers of the way of life that Jesus represented. In what follows, we can expect to find practical examples to guide us if we want to emulate those first believers.

Chapter One

Acting on Conviction
"We must obey God rather than men."

The book of Acts begins with Luke's recounting of the essentials of Jesus' last 40 days on earth (Acts 1:1–9). Christ had proven His resurrection from the dead by making several appearances to His disciples, giving them commands, and teaching them about the kingdom of God to come. Because Jesus had overcome a gruesome death perpetrated by the Romans, the disciples had understandably hoped that God's rule would be established immediately, ridding them of their oppressive pagan overlords. But Jesus told them that their attention had to be on the job at hand, not on the timing of the coming of God's kingdom. They were to wait in Jerusalem until the promised Holy Spirit from God the Father would be given to them. That spirit would empower them to accomplish great things around the world in service to Jesus, who would soon return to His Father. His disappearance from the earth by ascension from the Mount of Olives surely took them by surprise, despite the forewarning He had given them on the evening before His death (John 14:25–29; 16:16). But they were reassured by angelic beings that Jesus would return one day just as He had departed (Acts 1:10–11).

With these encouraging words in their ears, the disciples went back into Jerusalem. Together with Jesus' mother (Mary), His brothers and a number of women, they waited in a prayerful frame of mind as instructed. During their wait, at Peter's suggestion, they chose a replacement for Jesus' betrayer, Judas Iscariot, now dead by his own hand. Over the previous three years, various other men had become followers of Jesus. Some had recently witnessed Him as a resurrected being. Choosing two, the remaining eleven disciples asked for God's direction, and by the drawing of lots, Matthias was selected (Acts 1:12–26).

Chapter One: Acting on Conviction

Visitors to Jerusalem

On the Hebrew holy day *Shavuot* (the Feast of Weeks), about 10 days after Jesus' ascension, the disciples' wait was rewarded. Suddenly, in the early morning, the house in which they were gathered was shaken as if by a great rushing wind, and what looked like a tongue of fire rested above each one's head. Luke records that at that moment they were filled with the Holy Spirit and given the temporary ability to speak in other intelligible languages (Acts 2:1–4).

The Feast of Weeks, observed 50 days after the Passover season, was also known as Pentecost (meaning "count 50" in the language of the Septuagint—the Greek translation of the Hebrew Scriptures of that time). The holy day brought to Jerusalem many Jews and converts to Judaism from a wide geographic area. Luke mentions visitors from 15 different locations, from Parthia and Arabia to North Africa and Rome. When some of them heard the sound of the great wind, they gathered outside the house, wondering what was happening. They were even more surprised and perplexed when they heard many languages being spoken by the disciples. Each group was hearing in their own language what the apostles were explaining about God's great works. Some, not understanding these foreign languages, could only think that the speakers were drunk (Acts 2:5–13).

The audience that day was a microcosm of those to be reached by the good news that the apostle Peter was about to deliver. That the children of Israel, and in particular the branch known as Jews, would no longer be solely designated the people of God had been foreordained. The prophets of old had spoken of God as the God of the gentile peoples— that is, strangers to the children of Israel. Jesus' birth had been announced as bringing great joy "for *all* the people" (Luke 2:10, emphasis added). In his Gospel, Luke had given the account of the infant Jesus' blessing by Simeon. The man had referred to the baby as "a light for revelation to the Gentiles, and for glory to your people Israel" (see Luke 2:32 and Isaiah 42:6). Later, as an adult, Jesus had been recognized by Samaritans (who were much despised by Jews) as "the Savior of *the world*" (John 4:42, emphasis added). He had taught principally in "Galilee of the Gentiles" (Matthew 4:15), where the effect of East-West trade was felt as nations mingled and the cross-fertilization of ideas and cultures occurred. Just before His ascension, Jesus had commissioned the disciples to be witnesses to Him "to the end of the earth" (Acts 1:8; see also Matthew 28:19). And now on Pentecost, adherents to Judaism from many gentile lands, including Arabs (Acts 2:11), had been the first to hear about Jesus' death and resurrection and the coming of the Holy Spirit that day.

And yet as we will see, not all early followers of Jesus accepted that God was now opening the way for all humanity to come to know Him.

Peter's Message

Peter began his explanation by denying that he and his colleagues had had too much to drink—it was but nine in the morning. Rather, he said, an ancient Hebrew prophecy was being fulfilled. The ninth-century-B.C.E. prophet Joel had written of a day when God would "pour out [His] Spirit on all flesh." It would be the beginning of the final era of human history before the establishment of the kingdom of God on the earth (see Acts 2:17–21 and Joel 2:28–32). Peter said that the miraculous speaking in other languages was evidence of the coming of the Holy Spirit to humanity. He went on to explain in the boldest terms that the well-known miracle worker, Jesus of Nazareth, recently crucified by the Romans at the insistence of Jerusalem's Jewish religious leadership, was now alive by resurrection.

Perhaps acknowledging the Jewish tradition that King David had died on the Feast of Weeks a thousand years earlier, Peter reminded them that the monarch's tomb was there in Jerusalem for all to see. But Jesus, the son of David and the much anticipated Messiah, was alive from the dead, as the king himself had prophesied (Acts 2:22–32 and Psalm 16:8–11). Further, David's remains were still in his tomb; he was not in heaven. On the other hand, Jesus, whom they had crucified, *was* now there and had sent the Holy Spirit from the Father.

The audience was stung by the realization that they were complicit in the death of an innocent man, a man who had paid the ultimate penalty for their individual sins. They asked the apostles what they could do to make amends. Peter instructed them to be baptized by immersion in water as a token of their willingness to be washed clean of sin of all kinds, and to receive the gift of the Holy Spirit to help them live according to God's way (Acts 2:38). The same path would be open from that time on to all those whom God would call to an understanding of personal sin and the price that Jesus had paid for all.

The New Testament Church Flourishes

Because of God's calling, about three thousand people were baptized that day and joined with the apostles and other followers of Jesus. A new dynamism surged through the whole group, and as Luke says, "they devoted themselves to the apostles' teaching and the fellowship" (Acts 2:42). Miracles continued to be performed; people shared their goods so that none was in need. There was energy and conviction. The disciples were of one mind as they went about their daily lives, in the temple and visiting each other in their homes. The Church began to flourish.

It was at the temple that the young Church met its first challenge. The apostles Peter and John had gone there at the hour of prayer, three o'clock in the afternoon, and a congenitally lame man who regularly begged at one of the gates was there as usual. He asked Peter and John for money. Peter said, "Look at us. . . . I have no silver and gold, but what I do have I give to you. In the name of Jesus Christ of Nazareth, rise up and walk" (Acts 3:4, 6). Peter lifted him by the right hand and the man's feet and ankles were strengthened. He immediately leapt up and was able to walk. He caused a great stir among the people when he went into the temple and was recognized as the man who had been lame for more than 40 years.

The crowd's amazement provided Peter with the opportunity to explain what had happened and why. He repeated some of his Pentecost message, saying that his listeners were ignorantly complicit in the death of Jesus, and yet it was through faith in the resurrected Jesus' name that the lame man could now walk. What they needed was to change their way of living and be baptized, so that the penalty of their sins could be blotted out. He told them that Jesus Christ would return to the earth when the prophesied "times of restoration" (Acts 3:21, New King James Version) would be initiated. By that he meant the era when the kingdom of God will come to the earth and human rule will be replaced by godly rule. He reminded them that Moses had prophesied of the time when a great Prophet would come. That man, Peter said, was Jesus of Nazareth. Just as surely as His death had been prophesied and had happened, so His promised return would happen. Both events were to be understood as a blessing for *all humanity* (Acts 3:12–26).

The apostles were acting on what they believed, but the priests became upset when they heard them speak about Jesus and resurrection from the dead. By religious party affiliation, the priests were mostly Sadducees, who did not believe in a resurrection from the dead. Understandably, the group feared the apostles' influence over the people. Accompanied by the captain of the temple guard, they arrested Peter and John and imprisoned them till the next day, when the Jewish authorities questioned them. As for the people who had heard and responded to Peter and John, Luke says the number of men alone reached five thousand (either in total in Jerusalem or specifically because of Peter's speech). This was significant growth.

Called Into Question

When the high priest, his family and other leaders came together the following day as the Sanhedrin, or religious council, they asked the apostles by what power or in whose name they had healed the lame man. Peter boldly told the truth and reminded the same religious leaders who had sent Jesus to His death that it was because of His resurrection and faith in His name that the man was now able to walk. He also emphasized that there is no other name by which people may come to God and be saved (Acts 4:12).

Knowing they were trapped by the public's knowledge of the evident miracle, the Sanhedrin conferred and decided to curb the apostles by threatening them and forbidding them to speak in Jesus' name again. Peter and John stood their ground, insisting that they had to bear witness to what they knew to be true.

Allowed to go, they returned to their colleagues and together prayed that God would give them more boldness to speak His truth and to perform similar miracles. Again their meeting place was shaken and the Holy Spirit empowered them to be united in the work at hand, sharing their possessions readily. One man who freely donated the proceeds of a land sale was a Jewish Cypriot named Barnabas. Luke introduces us to this man as the "Son of Encouragement" (verse 36, NKJV). He was to play an important role in the spreading of the message beyond the land of the Jews.

Greed, Lies, Death and Healing

Luke contrasts Barnabas's example of generosity to that of Ananias and Sapphira. This couple had also decided to sell property and had pledged all the proceeds as an offering to the Church, yet had then held back part of the money. The result, once Peter had met with them separately, was their immediate collapse and death. It was a powerful warning to the Church not to renege on commitments to God (Acts 5:1–11).

At the same time, the apostles' reputation for miracles was growing, so much that the physically and mentally ill were brought from miles around Jerusalem. This did not escape the attention of the high priest and his Saducean party. Soon Peter and the apostles were back in prison, only to escape by angelic intervention during the night. By morning, unknown to the religious authorities, they were back in the temple obeying God's order to speak out boldly "all the words of this Life" (verse 20). Again we learn that it is a way of life, a practical path that is being taught.

When the officers came to the prison to bring the apostles before the high priest, they were astonished to find their cell empty, though the guarded door was still locked. Someone came with the news that the freed men were in the temple teaching once more. Now the authorities brought the apostles back to the council without violence for fear of the people. Questioned about their disobedience to the earlier ruling not to teach about Jesus and the rulers' role in His death, the apostles responded even more directly that God was the one they would heed, not the murderers of Jesus. Peter and the others answered, "We must obey God rather than men" (verse 29). It is a vital principle, based in practical obedience to God when the other choice is to follow human rulings that contradict God's commands.

The council was furious and began to devise ways to kill the apostles. But the wisdom of one council member, a respected Pharisee and teacher of the law named Gamaliel, prevailed. He counseled that if the apostles were of God, then it would be foolish to oppose them; but if they were indeed merely men without God's backing, then they would fail anyway. Just as previous troublemakers such as Theudas and Judas of Galilee had come to nothing after they had started popular new movements, so waiting out these men was wise. The council agreed and, having beaten the apostles and again prohibited their speaking in Jesus' name, set them free once more (verses 33–42).

Practical Concerns

As the Church continued to develop, certain practical challenges occurred within. One concerned what appears to have been a case of discrimination against widows who were Greek-speaking. It seems that the provision of funds or daily food among the followers in Jerusalem was unequal, with Hebrew-speaking widows receiving preferential treatment. The dispute needed the apostles' attention. Their decision was not to resolve the matter themselves but rather to have the congregation bring forward the names of seven respected men whom the apostles could appoint to take care of such organizational matters.

Chosen for what was later to become the role of deacon—a capable local leader—were seven men known by reputation to be full of the Holy Spirit and wisdom. Significantly, all had Greek names, and the last listed was non-Jewish, a convert to Judaism from Antioch in Syria. They were Stephen, Philip, Prochorus, Nicanor, Timon, Parmenas and Nicolas. The apostles wisely agreed that men with these characteristics would be least likely to discriminate against any of the widows. Once they prayed and laid hands upon the men, thereby conferring authority to do the work at hand, the Church in Jerusalem no longer experienced the problem and began to grow in numbers again. Even some members of the priesthood joined with them (Acts 6:1–7).

Stephen's Witness

One of the most significant shifts in the spread of the gospel message in early New Testament times came through the testimony of one of these seven men. While apostles led the work of the early Church, it was because of Stephen, "a [leading] man full of faith and of the Holy Spirit," that the world beyond Judea and Samaria began to hear the good news.

Stephen continued to grow in reputation and ability, but in Jerusalem he came into conflict with some members of a community known as the Synagogue of the Freedmen. They were Greek-speaking converts to Judaism, former Roman slaves who had won their freedom legally. They came from Egypt, North Africa, Cilicia and Asia Minor.

As a Greek-speaker himself, Stephen attracted the attention of the Freedmen, and they began to argue with him. But Stephen's spiritual capacities and wisdom proved too much for them, so they turned to false accusations and witnesses. Having succeeded in getting him arrested and brought before the Sanhedrin, they accused him of blasphemy against God, Moses, the temple and the law. They claimed that he taught that Jesus of Nazareth would destroy the temple and change the practices that Moses had taught (verses 8–14).

The high priest called on Stephen to answer the charges against him. His defense took the form of a short history of God's dealing with the patriarchs of ancient Israel. This allowed him to deny both charges by supporting Moses' role as deliverer of the Israelites and by showing that while God had promoted the building of two kinds of structure for worship (tabernacle and temple), He is not limited to dwelling in such places. Stephen showed how God had chosen Abraham and his descendants, the children of Jacob/Israel; how He had brought them into Egypt to be saved from famine; and how He had delivered them once more—this time from slavery—by the hand of Moses, whom the people nevertheless rejected on their wilderness journey. Showing the progression from tabernacle to temple in the worship of God, Stephen also emphasized that God is not to be confined to a building. In some ways, the Jewish religious leadership had allowed the temple to supersede God in their affections (Acts 6:15–7:50).

Stephen ended with a searing conclusion, drawing a parallel between his audience and their rebellious ancestors. He said that their forefathers had rejected evidence of the Holy Spirit at work in Moses, their deliverer, and in the prophets, whom their fathers had murdered. In the same way the present leadership had rejected the Holy Spirit at work in the Messiah and Deliverer, Jesus of Nazareth, whom they had murdered. The implication was that they, not Stephen, were the ones guilty of blasphemy. They had rejected the power of God at work in Jesus and conspired to murder Him. Stephen's words enraged the council, who glared in fury at their accuser. But Stephen looked up and saw a vision of God's throne with Jesus standing by the Father. The council members dragged Stephen outside the city and, in an illegal act, stoned him to death (Acts 7:51–59). His last words were similar to Christ's own at His crucifixion: "Lord, do not hold this sin against them" (verse 60). Thus Stephen became the first martyr in the New Testament Church.

Stephen's death was agreed to and observed by a man who was also to become a major player in the furtherance of the Church's mission—Saul of Tarsus, known better as the apostle Paul (Acts 22:20).

Saul himself soon became involved in a fierce attack on the entire Church (Acts 8:1–3). This intensified persecution caused many of Jesus' followers, except the apostles, to flee from Jerusalem to outlying areas in Judea and Samaria—some even going up the coast to Phoenicia, to Antioch in Northern Syria, and to Cyprus (Acts 8:4, 11:19–22). Stephen's death became a catalyst for more persecution, but at the same time it caused a sudden acceleration and expansion of the message of and about Jesus, as fleeing members of the Church told of their experiences and faith.

Philip of the Seven

One of those who went out from Jerusalem following Stephen's death was his colleague, Philip, another of the seven chosen to help the Jerusalem widows. Luke refers to him later as "Philip the evangelist" (Acts 21:8). This man went to Samaria and taught about Jesus and the kingdom of God (Acts 8:12).

The Samaritans were disliked by the Jews, who would have little to do with them. This was in part because the Samaritans claimed to be descendants of the children of Israel. They had also adopted the first five books of the Hebrew Scriptures, the Pentateuch, and taught that their own enclave at nearby Mount Gerizim, rather than Jerusalem, was the place to worship God. The Jews believed them to be descendants of colonists brought in centuries earlier by the Assyrians, who created a blend of pagan and Hebrew religion (see 2 Kings 17:24–41). Significantly, Samaria was one of the first places where the gospel was delivered by the early Church, showing that the message was meant for all humanity and that traditional animosities would not prevent Jesus' teachings becoming available to all.

Philip's ministry in Samaria was confirmed by miraculous healings, which in turn attracted a well-known

Samaritan sorcerer. Simon Magus, as he is known to history, was a powerful figure and leader of a group influenced by ideas that later became known as Gnosticism. The Samaritans were in awe of his works of magic and esteemed him as "the power of God that is called Great" (Acts 8:9–10).

Along with others of his countrymen, Simon was baptized by Philip. The apostles, who had remained in Jerusalem, heard the news about Philip's success and sent two of their number, Peter and John, to visit the new converts. On arrival, they learned that the Samaritan believers had not yet received the Holy Spirit. They then prayed for them and laid their hands on their heads so that the gift could be given.

When Simon the magician saw that the apostles were used to confer the Holy Spirit, he offered them money so that he could do the same for others. This was a clear sign to Peter that Simon was not converted and that his interest lay in having power over people. Peter's reply was unequivocal: "May your silver perish with you, because you thought you could obtain the gift of God with money! You have neither part nor lot in this matter, for your heart is not right before God" (verses 20–21). He went on to say that Simon should repent, poisoned as he was by bitterness and captive to evil. Simon's response was not that he wanted to repent, rather that the apostles should pray for him. But the apostles simply returned to Jerusalem, visiting and speaking in other Samaritan villages on the way.

Philip and the Ethiopian

Philip's next assignment after visiting Samaria was to go to the desert area close to Gaza (verse 26). There he came upon a government official from Ethiopia, the treasurer of Queen Candace. He happened to be what the New Testament terms a "God-fearer"—someone who was committed to God and who attended the synagogue, though not a full member of the Jewish faith. He had been in Jerusalem and was now returning home.

When Philip met him, he was sitting in his chariot reading a section from the writings of Isaiah. Philip asked whether he understood what he was reading. The Ethiopian replied that he could not unless someone would teach him, and he asked Philip to join him. Together they discussed a passage that speaks prophetically of Jesus Christ's sacrificial death (see Isaiah 53:7–8). The Ethiopian then knew what he needed to do and asked Philip to baptize him, professing his belief in Jesus as the Messiah.

After being immersed in water, the man "went on his way rejoicing" (Acts 8:39), and Philip disappeared, being found later at Ashdod, north of Gaza. There he continued preaching, traveling along the coast till he came to the Roman port of Caesarea, where he probably took up residence (see Acts 21:8).

What is so striking about this section of Acts is that it confirms again that the spread of the gospel message was not limited in any way. Here, at an early point, an African worshiper of God became part of the New Testament Church with the help of a Greek-speaking Jew. That his helper was not principally Hebrew-speaking and that the 12 apostles were still focused on Jerusalem, despite the commission Jesus had given them to go into all the world (see Mark 16:15), is a telling point. But the dissemination of the truth about Jesus Christ and His message was not going to be held back.

An Astonishing Change of Heart

Meanwhile the Pharisee Saul, who had witnessed Stephen's death, intensified his efforts to rid the region of the followers of Jesus. "Breathing threats and murder," he gained written permission from the high priest in Jerusalem to go to Damascus, where he suspected the Jewish community was welcoming followers of the Way. He intended to bring any such men and women "bound to Jerusalem" (Acts 9:1-2). As Saul neared Damascus, he was suddenly overcome by a great light from heaven and fell to the ground. He heard Jesus' voice asking why he was persecuting Him. Jesus then told him to go into Damascus, where he would learn more.

Saul's companions had heard the voice but saw no one. When Saul got up from the ground, he could see nothing. He was led on foot into the city, where he spent the next three days sightless and fasting. It was then that a disciple of Jesus, named Ananias, received instructions in a vision to seek out Saul and help him to recover his sight. Saul was praying and had been told, also in a vision, that a man named Ananias would come to him. Ananias was understandably confused by his task, knowing that Saul was a fierce persecutor of his fellow believers in Jerusalem, newly arrived in Damascus to hunt down more of them. Jesus' reply was "Go, for he is a chosen instrument of mine to carry my name before the Gentiles and kings and the children of Israel. For I will show him how much he must suffer for the sake of my name" (verses 15-16). Saul was about to become one of the most effective servants of the gospel, a persecutor no more.

Finding the repentant Saul, Ananias laid hands upon him so that his sight could be restored and he could receive the Holy Spirit. As suddenly as he had lost his sight, he regained it and was baptized. The effect on Saul was electric. After a few days in Damascus with the disciples, he visited the local synagogues, testifying and proving that Jesus is the Messiah. His listeners were nothing short of amazed at this reversal, knowing who he was and why he had come.

Eventually, however, the effects of Saul's conversion brought him into such contention with some of the Jews that they set out to kill him. Once he became aware of the plot, he was able to escape by night with the help of the disciples, who let him down through the city wall in a large basket. Returning to Jerusalem, he attempted to associate with the disciples there but immediately found himself unwelcome. Not only were the believers afraid of the man who had persecuted their families and friends and had agreed to the stoning of Stephen, their beloved helper, but they also did not accept that he was a genuine convert.

It took the efforts of the much-trusted disciple Barnabas to persuade the followers to accept Saul. He began by taking him to the apostles, who, hearing the former persecutor's account of his Damascus Road experience and all that had happened in that city, recognized that a miracle had occurred. Saul was accepted among them. But again his new identity brought him under attack. Disputing with other Greek-speaking Jews in Jerusalem, who soon became antagonistic to the point of threatening his life, he had to flee. The believers helped him and brought him to the port city of Caesarea, where he took a ship northward to Cilicia and his hometown of Tarsus.

At this point in the book of Acts, Saul disappears for several years. In the meantime the churches in Judea, Galilee and Samaria develop in peace and grow in numbers, with Peter taking a leading role in their establishment.

Chapter Two

Peter, Paul and Barnabas

"God has shown me that I should not call any person common or unclean."

During the apostle Peter's early ministry, people were convinced about Jesus' Messiahship by the evidence of miraculous healings. Two such incidents occurred when Peter visited Church members along the Mediterranean coast of central Palestine. In Lydda (Lod), he met a paralyzed man named Aeneas, who had been bedridden for eight years. At Peter's word the man got to his feet and was healed. This convinced many in Lydda and the Sharon area to become followers of Jesus.

In nearby Joppa (Jaffa), a disciple named Tabitha, or Dorcas, was also the recipient of a miracle. She was known among the believers for her good works and charitable deeds. But she died while Peter was at Lydda. The disciples sent for him and brought him to the room where her body lay. Peter sent everyone out of the room and prayed over her, telling her to rise. She sat up, took his hand and stood. Luke notes that Peter then presented her to the saints and widows. (In the New Testament, the term *saint* refers not to a person who has undergone an elaborate investigation of his or her works, followed by veneration, beatification and canonization, but simply to those God has called into His Church. They are sanctified, or set apart, for service to God by living His way of life. They are ordinary people with an extraordinary calling.) Dorcas had been a helper and servant to the widows and the other members, and they were very appreciative of her coming back to life. The miracle became well known in the region, and more were added to the Church.

A Centurion Becomes a Follower

Peter stayed in Joppa for several days at the house of Simon the Tanner. According to Old Testament law, Simon's work made him ceremonially unclean because he handled the skins of dead animals (Leviticus 11:39–40). But Peter was not averse to staying with him, being willing to associate with people perhaps shunned by others. It was a helpful attitude, bearing in mind what was about to happen with the Roman centurion Cornelius, who lived about 33 miles (53 kilometers) away in Caesarea, the Roman capital of Judea.

Cornelius and his men were part of the large Italian Regiment stationed in the port city. Like many non-Jews in the first century, he and his household had become God-fearers—worshipers of the God of Israel. The centurion had a vision telling him that God had heard his prayers and noted his charitable works, and that he should send to Joppa for Peter, who would tell him what he should do (Acts 10:1–6).

As Cornelius's servants and one of his God-fearing soldiers approached the town, Peter was praying on the rooftop of Simon's house. He became very hungry, and falling into a trance, he saw a great sheet tied at the four corners coming down to him out of heaven, filled with all kinds of animals including reptiles and birds. A voice told him to rise, kill and eat. Knowing that the sheet contained many animals that the Hebrew Scriptures designate as unfit to eat—"unclean" meats—Peter refused. The voice from heaven said, "What God has made clean, do not call common" (verses 9–15).

This happened three times and left Peter puzzling about the meaning. Many commentators assert that it was God's way of telling Peter that the food laws of the Old Testament had become obsolete. Nothing could be further from the truth. Peter's explanation of what he derived from the experience is found just a few verses later. He said to

Cornelius, "God has shown me that I should not call any *person* common or unclean" (verse 28, emphasis added). There is not a hint of any change in the food laws. It would have seemed very odd to Cornelius, the God-fearer, whose belief was informed by devotion to the God of Israel and whose guide was the Hebrew Scriptures, to meet a Jew whose message was in part a rescinding of the food laws.

At the request of Cornelius's servants, Peter and some of the disciples from Joppa went to his house. There Peter recognized that God was opening the door of salvation to the gentiles, just as he had to the Jews. Here was a God-fearing man with his relatives and close friends, anxious to know what God would have them do (verses 24–33). As Peter delivered his message about Jesus' life, death and resurrection, the Holy Spirit came on the household. Peter instantly knew what was taking place, no doubt recalling what had happened to him on Pentecost, about 10 years earlier, when the Holy Spirit had been given to the apostles. He then instructed that Cornelius and his household be baptized for the forgiveness of their sins. Like the Jewish apostles and witnesses to Jesus' ministry, the gentile centurion had become a follower of the Way (verses 34–48).

When Peter returned to Jerusalem, the six disciples who had accompanied him to Caesarea were his witnesses to what had happened. The apostle met with opposition from some of the Jewish believers, who accused him of defiling himself by eating with gentile Romans. Peter and the witnesses told their story and convinced the Jerusalem church that God had indeed made His truth and way of life available to all humanity. It was a significant step forward in accomplishing the commission that Jesus had given His disciples: "Go therefore and make disciples of all nations, . . . teaching them to observe all that I have commanded you" (Matthew 28:19–20).

Events in Syrian Antioch

Following the murder of Stephen and the persecution led by Saul against the followers of Jesus in Jerusalem (Acts 7:54–60; 8:1, 3), many had escaped to other parts of the region. They had gone to outlying areas in Judea and Samaria, and some to Phoenicia, to Cyprus, and to Antioch in northern Syria (Acts 8:1, 4; 11:19–22). They had talked to others about their new beliefs, but their listeners were exclusively Jews. Some believers who came originally from Cyprus and Cyrene in North Africa had gone to Antioch. In this great crossroads city, the third-largest in the Roman Empire after Rome and Alexandria, they had told Greek-speakers—who were probably neither Jews nor gentile proselytes to Judaism, though possibly God-fearers—about Jesus of Nazareth. As a result, "a great number who believed turned to the Lord" (Acts 11:21). The account's position in the story of the spread of the good news adds weight to the probability that these people were not Jewish. As we have just seen, what immediately precedes it is the conversion of gentiles in Palestine and their acceptance by the Jerusalem church.

As a result of the sudden growth in the Antioch congregation, the believers in Jerusalem sent one of their leaders, Barnabas, to discover what exactly had happened. His visit soon confirmed the truth of what they had heard, and as a result of his encouraging teaching and enthusiasm, more were added to the Church (verse 24). Barnabas was not unfamiliar with such unexpected developments in the Church's work. He had been able to introduce the apostles in Jerusalem to the repentant persecutor Saul and tell them of his astonishing conversion on the Damascus Road and his work in the synagogues there.

Now with the growth in Antioch, Barnabas realized he needed help and set out to find Saul once more. Recall that Saul (or to use his Roman name, Paul) had left Palestine some 10 years earlier to escape Greek-speaking Jews who opposed his newfound faith. What exactly he did during that decade is not known for sure, though he writes that after his conversion he went to Syria and Cilicia (Galatians 1:21; see also Acts 15:23, 41). By the time Barnabas found him, he was ready to help in Antioch. Luke tells us that Barnabas and Paul worked together in the city for a year, meeting with the church, "and taught a great many people" (Acts 11:26).

We also learn that it was in Antioch that "the disciples were first called Christians." This is a statement that cannot be taken at face value. The conclusion that most draw is that the term *Christian* is the biblical name for the followers of Christ. Yet the New Testament uses it in only two other places (Acts 26:28 and 1 Peter 4:16), and in no case is it a self-description. As various scholars note, it was a term used derisively by others for the followers of Jesus. In the earliest New Testament times, several terms were used by Church members of themselves, including *brethren, disciples, believers, saints, followers of the Way* and *Church of God*. It was only in the second century that some were willing to accept the term *Christian,* but in so doing they ignored early Church understanding and practice.

Events in Jerusalem

While Barnabas and Paul were working in Antioch, prophets came from Jerusalem, and one of them, Agabus, announced that there would be a great famine. Luke records that this actually occurred in the days of Claudius Caesar, who ruled from 41–54 C.E. The disciples in Antioch believed the prophecy and collected relief money to send to the Jerusalem elders with Barnabas and Paul.

Subsequent events in Jerusalem help us date the famine fairly accurately. Acts 12 opens with an account of the attack on the church there by King Herod Agrippa (11 B.C.E.–44 C.E.). First he killed James the brother of John, one of the original disciples of Jesus, and then he jailed the apostle Peter during the spring holy day season known as the Passover and Days of Unleavened Bread (verses 1–4). Some versions of the New Testament wrongly refer to this season as "Easter," a word that does not appear in the original Greek text.

Because of the king's persecution, the local congregation was in a state of constant prayer for the imprisoned Peter. Suddenly during the night, he was miraculously freed. Arriving at the home of a woman named Mary (the mother of Barnabas's cousin John Mark, author of the Gospel of Mark [verse 12; Colossians 4:10]), where the brethren were gathered together, Peter knocked. The young woman who answered the gate was so happy to see him that she failed to open it, running back inside to tell the others. They simply dismissed her words as impossible, telling her she was mad or had seen an angel—this despite the fact that what they were intently praying for had happened (verses 5–18). Sometimes we do not recognize the answer to prayer when it comes!

An End and a Beginning

Herod for his part, having failed to recapture Peter, went down to Caesarea. There his life came to an abrupt end. He had been angry with the people of the port cities of Tyre and Sidon, who now sued for peace. Herod set a day aside to meet with them, and after they had heard his speech, they acclaimed him a god. Because Herod failed to deny the adulation and give glory to God, Luke records that an angel struck him with a disease, and that he died, having been eaten by worms. History records Herod's death in 44 C.E., and the Jewish historian Josephus mentions that it came after five days of stomach pains. Meanwhile, Luke writes that in the Church "the word of God increased and multiplied" (verses 19–24).

Apparently present in Jerusalem during this time, Barnabas and Paul delivered the relief funds, and taking John Mark with them, they returned to Antioch.

In that city there were several prophets and teachers. Besides Barnabas and Paul, there was Simeon, possibly a black man judging by his Latin surname, Niger. There was another from North Africa, Lucius of Cyrene, and Manaen, who had grown up with Herod Antipas.

It was among this group, as they were praying and fasting, that the inspiration came to send Barnabas and Paul on a new journey that was to initiate a major phase in the further spread of the gospel message and the opening of the world to the west. It was the first of several journeys that Paul would make over the next two decades to what would become the new arena for the good news.

At Antioch in Syria, a flourishing congregation was well established by the time Barnabas and Paul were selected to expand their teaching activities. The support of the followers of Jesus meant much to the two men, and they would return to their home base to report on their experiences. The pair set out with Barnabas's relative John Mark as a helper. Together they went down to the Roman port of Seleucia, about 16 miles (25 kilometers) away, to take a ship to the island of Cyprus. Sailing southwest about 135 miles (about 220 kilometers), they would have arrived in the pristine waters of the eastern Cypriot city of Salamis after just a few hours.

From Synagogue to Sorcerer

Cyprus was a natural first stop on their journey, since Barnabas was a native of the island (Acts 4:36), and others had preceded them following the persecution and dispersion of the Church in Jerusalem after the martyring of Stephen (Acts 11:19). Paul, of course, had been actively opposed to the believers and instrumental in Stephen's murder and the scattering of the group. He surely was mindful of the origins of his faith as they stepped ashore and he considered the work ahead.

Facing the coastline just to the north of Palestine, Salamis had long attracted Jewish people, probably beginning in the Greek period (fourth to first century B.C.E.), when it was the island's principal city. In the first century C.E., the city was still the major commercial center on the island. The Jewish Diaspora community had several well-established synagogues.

It was there that the three travelers went first. This was to become the pattern in Paul's teaching: Initially he would go to the synagogue, where according to some scholars the

Diaspora audience was as much as 50 percent non-Jewish in the first-century. He would speak to his fellow Jews, proselytes and the God-fearers among them. He would tell them that the Messiah had come and then prove it from the Hebrew Scriptures. After all, these were the people with whom he had a common background. If Paul's message had contradicted the Hebrew writings and traditional worship, no one would have listened.

Nothing more is recorded of this stay in Salamis, though we know that later Barnabas returned to Cyprus with John Mark—apparently to encourage the believers already established there (Acts 15:36–39).

The three men went next to the western side of the island, to the city of Paphos, which had become the Roman administrative capital and was the first port of call in Cyprus for vessels sailing eastward through the Mediterranean. It was to be a very significant visit. Here they came in contact with the governor of the island, the Roman proconsul Sergius Paulus. The name has been found in three Roman inscriptions, one of which identifies a curator of the River Tiber in Rome near the time that Barnabas and Paul would have visited Cyprus.

Sergius Paulus called for the visitors and was especially impressed when Paul showed the governor's spiritual advisor, the Jewish magician Bar-Jesus, to be a fraud. The man had opposed the travelers and tried to dissuade the governor from accepting their teaching. Paul called on God to temporarily blind the magician so that he would learn not to be an enemy. When Bar-Jesus asked to be led by the hand, Sergius Paulus was convinced and became a believer in God's power and Paul's message.

The governor probably came from another city named Antioch, this one in the Pisidia region in central Asia Minor, where according to recent scholarship his family owned large amounts of land. It was to this city that Barnabas and Paul would travel next. Did the proconsul suggest that they go to his home area to deliver their message to his family? After all, his relatives could have given help and support and contacts in the Roman colony. It seems a good enough reason for Paul and his party to have sailed from Paphos to Perga on what is today the southern Turkish coast.

Success in a Roman Setting

In Perga, we are told, John Mark left his companions and returned to Jerusalem. With their helper gone, the men began the difficult journey from Perga north across the challenging Taurus Mountains to Pisidian Antioch, about 3,600 feet (1,100 meters) above sea level. For much of the time since the city's founding around 280 B.C.E., Jews had lived there. It was a Roman administrative center in Galatia, which had been named a Roman province in 25 B.C.E. by the emperor Augustus. By Paul's time, some of the inhabitants were descendants of Roman veterans who had been allowed to retire there. It was a city under significant construction—so much so that its magnificence was said by some to resemble that of Rome.

When Paul and Barnabas arrived in the city, Luke tells us that "on the Sabbath day they went into the synagogue" (Acts 13:14). The leaders of the congregation asked the Jewish visitors to speak to the people. Once again the synagogue community Paul visited was both Jewish and gentile. It is important to note here that many in the Roman

Empire were impressed with Judaism, which was regarded as a very old religion—perhaps even the primary religion. Many adopted the Hebrew God, Yahweh, and Judaism was granted special religious liberties in some parts of the empire—including freedom to worship on the Sabbath. So it would not have been so strange to find non-Jewish Romans in synagogues outside Judea. This explains why Paul addressed the audience in Antioch as "sons of the family of Abraham, and those among you who fear God [the gentile God-fearers]" (verse 26). Here is a clear indication that Paul was speaking to two distinct groups—some of the same kinds of people that formed the Church in other parts of the Diaspora.

His discourse about the history of ancient Israel and the life, death and resurrection of Jesus was so effective that some Jews and proselytes and/or God-fearers joined with him. Others asked that the same message be given to them the next Sabbath, when we are told that "almost the whole city gathered to hear the word of the Lord" (verse 44).

What Paul taught has been the subject of much debate. Some are convinced that he spoke against keeping the law and in favor of "living under grace." But if Paul had taught against the law, would he have been able to convince Jews in the synagogue, who became followers of Jesus, not to keep the Sabbath, for example? Would he have taught Jewish and gentile believers to follow different practices? Would Paul have asked the Jews to meet on the Sabbath and the gentiles to meet separately on Sunday? How could the Church ever have come together on that basis? How could the Church ever have been united in belief and practice? They could not, and indeed Paul refers to the Jewish and gentile followers of Jesus in Corinth in the singular as "the church of God," not as two different groups with different beliefs and practices (see 1 Corinthians 10:32). The only logical conclusion is that he taught both elements in the Church the same thing, including assembling together on the same day—the Sabbath.

Violent Opposition Begins

The Jews who did not accept Paul's message were envious of his success and spoke against him (Acts 13:45). This had the effect of convincing Paul that in this place he should now teach only gentiles. Again he was successful, and word spread throughout the region. More animosity from the unbelieving Jews, who stirred up the city leaders and some of the God-fearing wealthy women supporters of the synagogue, caused the two apostles to be thrown out of the area.

From Antioch, Paul and Barnabas traveled southeast about 90 miles (145 kilometers) to Iconium (modern Konya) in what was anciently the province of Phrygia. It had become part of Galatia in 25 B.C.E. At the time of Paul's visit, it was probably a Greek city and not yet a Roman colony, though the emperor Claudius allowed it to be named Claudiconium after him. It was connected to Antioch by a Roman road, known as the Via Sebaste. Paul went to Iconium more than once during his ministry and wrote one of his New Testament letters to the congregations in the surrounding area of Galatia.

On the first visit, Paul and Barnabas went into the synagogue as usual, and many Jews and gentiles were convinced by their message. But in reaction, the remaining

Jews became upset and poisoned the minds of the other gentiles against the new believers. In spite of this strong opposition, Paul and Barnabas kept on teaching for quite some time. It was only when a violent plot against them was discovered that they fled for their lives to avoid being stoned (Acts 14:1–6).

Treated Like Gods, Then Left for Dead

The next two cities on Paul and Barnabas's journey, Lystra and Derbe in Lycaonia, were reached by an unpaved road. Today there's virtually nothing to be seen of these cities, just mounds of debris where they may have been.

When Paul healed a crippled man who sat by the gates of Lystra, it caused a public sensation. The onlookers were convinced that the gods had come down to them. This was an audience unlike others Paul and Barnabas had encountered. They were pagans, believers in the Greek gods. Just outside the city was a temple dedicated to Zeus, father of the gods. The people took Barnabas to be Zeus, and Paul, Hermes, since in Greek mythology it was he who accompanied Zeus and was his messenger. The local priest of Zeus immediately responded, arriving with garlands and oxen to offer a sacrifice to the visitors.

Paul and Barnabas were shocked by the adulation and ran in among the people to dissuade them, explaining that they were just men (verses 14–15). The situation gave Paul the opportunity to craft his message in a new way, one that he would repeat with other pagan audiences. He told them that there was a living God, maker of all creation. This God was different from their powerless "vanities" and in the past had allowed all nations to follow their own ways. Yet He did not fail to make Himself known to humanity in that He did good by giving "rains from heaven and fruitful seasons, satisfying your hearts with food and gladness" (verses 15–17). Paul's words were only barely sufficient to prevent the emotionally charged Lystrians from completing their sacrificial offering.

Soon trouble of a more serious kind emerged with the arrival of enemy Jews from Antioch and Iconium, who had heard about events in Lystra. They now led the people in an attempt on Paul's life. They stoned him and left him for dead outside the city. The few who had responded to Paul's message stood around his body—no doubt including a young man named Timothy (who was to become Paul's "beloved and faithful child in the Lord" [1 Corinthians 4:17]) and members of his family. But Paul miraculously got up and went into the city.

From there he and Barnabas departed the next day for Derbe, where Luke tells us simply that they preached the gospel and taught many. Following this visit, Paul and Barnabas retraced their steps, strengthening the new believers and appointing elders to take care of the new churches. Arriving back at Perga, they preached once more and soon boarded a ship bound for their home base at Antioch in Syria.

A Make-or-Break Crisis

Once back in Syrian Antioch, they reported to the church all that had happened and how God "had opened a door of faith to the Gentiles" (verse 27). For about the next two and a half years they remained there, and it seems that the church was flourishing. But with the arrival of visitors from

Jerusalem another serious controversy began to develop. The matter of what Paul was teaching, especially to the gentile believers, now came to a head. It was to become a major discussion in the New Testament Church, one that required a visit to Jerusalem and a council decision. What exactly was the issue?

The church in Syrian Antioch was a very mixed group, comprising people from various ethnic and religious backgrounds. But despite their physical and cultural differences, as members of the Church of God, they were united in their belief. Then some men came from Judea and began to upset their peace. They were likely followers of Jesus, but probably also from the sect of the Pharisees. Though they had no instructions from Jerusalem to do so, they demanded circumcision of gentile followers of the Way. They said, "Unless you are circumcised according to the custom of Moses, you cannot be saved" (Acts 15:1).

Though Paul was also a Pharisee and Barnabas a Levite, they had not required circumcision of the gentile people they had taught, nor had the church in Syrian Antioch made any such demand. The argument could not be easily settled, so Paul and Barnabas were sent to confer with the apostles and elders in Jerusalem and to seek a decision. They were received positively when they reported how the Church had developed among the gentiles. But again, contention arose. "Some believers who belonged to the party of the Pharisees rose up and said, 'It is necessary to circumcise them and to order them to keep the law of Moses'" (verse 5). These men were also insisting that gentiles be circumcised so that the Pharisaic approach to the law of Moses could be maintained.

Coming To Agreement

After much debate, first Peter, then Barnabas and Paul recounted from their own experiences what had happened over the years in the developing Church as gentiles had come to belief in Jesus. They confirmed that such people had received the Holy Spirit without undergoing adult circumcision. In effect, their "circumcision" was of the heart. The sign by which God accepted them as equals with Jews was not physical but spiritual: they had the same Spirit-led mind.

When the audience had no more to say, James, the brother of Jesus and leader of the Jerusalem church, summarized and made a binding decision. Quoting the prophet Amos and relying on related statements from Isaiah and other Hebrew Scriptures, James showed that God's purpose is not limited to the people of Israel but includes "the rest of mankind" (verse 17, NKJV). Any thought of a rift between Paul and Peter or Paul and James over the controversy is shown by this account to be without basis in fact.

Thus the apostles and elders in Jerusalem decided that adult gentiles did not have to be circumcised. What Paul and Barnabas had taught was upheld as correct. The Jerusalem church also decided that the gentiles should be especially aware of four issues in their societies. They should "abstain from the things polluted by idols, and from sexual immorality, and from what has been strangled, and from blood" (verses 20, 29).

What is often missed is that these four prohibitions came from the time of Moses and governed the entry of gentiles into the nation of Israel. They were in that respect part of the

Mosaic law. There is no indication in the book of Acts that the gentiles should not keep the law. What had happened with respect to circumcision was simply a clarification of how the law of Moses would be applied to gentiles entering the community of the Church.

When Barnabas and Paul returned to Antioch, accompanied by two leading members of the Jerusalem church named Judas and Silas, there was joy that the teaching had been upheld.

Chapter Three

New Team, New Territory

At Troas, Paul had a dream in which he saw a Macedonian man pleading that they come over to his region. The dream was understood to be God's way of guiding their footsteps to an entirely new area for spreading the good news.

As Paul and his colleague Barnabas prepared to set out again from Syrian Antioch, they came to a serious disagreement over the future use of their assistant, John Mark. As noted earlier, Mark had accompanied them on their first extended trip together to Cyprus and into Asia Minor. But for reasons that are unclear, he had left them and returned home to Jerusalem.

That Paul was displeased with the attitude displayed by this action now becomes clear: when planning their next tour, he "thought best not to take with them one who had withdrawn from them in Pamphylia and had not gone with them to the work" (Acts 15:38). Barnabas seemed more inclined to be forgiving of his cousin and let bygones be bygones. The difference of opinion became so strong that Paul and Barnabas parted company, each man standing his ground and demonstrating as much by his choice of future traveling companion. Barnabas took John Mark and left Antioch for his home island of Cyprus. Paul chose Silas and began a tour of the congregations in Roman Syria and Cilicia, his home territory.

Temporary Disagreement

Some have puzzled over this impasse between men of God who had achieved so much together. It's important to note at the outset that their disagreement was not a matter of doctrine. It wasn't that one man began to teach something contrary or unbiblical. Their difference was over an administrative matter. It was about the choice of a traveling companion. Neither man departed from the faith nor from doing his part in the work at hand. The result of their disagreement was that they simply set out to serve the members of the *same* church in different areas. If Paul and Silas had gone to Cyprus instead, the people there would have heard the same message. Administrative separation seems to have been the wisest course of action in the circumstances. Personalities can clash even within the same belief structure, but the same work can still be accomplished until resolution is possible. If doctrine had been the issue, then separation would have become necessary in a more profound sense. And Paul and Barnabas could not have later found reconciliation without one stepping down and admitting doctrinal error.

What do we know of the men involved in this upset as time passed? In two of his later letters Paul writes, "If [Mark] comes to you, welcome him" (Colossians 4:10) and "Get Mark and bring him with you, for he is very useful to me for ministry" (2 Timothy 4:11). It seems obvious that reconciliation between Paul and Mark had occurred. But what of Barnabas? In Paul's first letter to the Corinthians, written a number of years after the disagreement, Paul clearly recognizes him as a fellow apostle (1 Corinthians 9:6). We can surely conclude that Paul reconciled with Barnabas and that the latter had been justified in his confidence in Mark.

A Wise Decision

As Paul and Silas continued their travels, they went from Cilicia through the steep-sided pass known as the Cilician Gates and came to the cities of Derbe and Lystra (Acts 16:1). There they met the disciple Timothy, who had apparently become a follower of Jesus during Paul's previous visit to Lystra and had developed a good reputation among the other members in the city and in neighboring Iconium.

It was well known among the Jews that Timothy's father was Greek and his mother Jewish. But Timothy was not circumcised—a reason for the local Jews to reject him. Because Paul intended to use Timothy as an assistant in the area, he had the young man undergo the procedure to combat Jewish prejudice. Part of the teaching that Paul and Silas brought to the congregations as they traveled was the decision made by the apostles and elders at Jerusalem two years earlier in respect of circumcision. They had confirmed that the physical ritual was no longer required of those entering a relationship with the God of Israel. But Paul knew that Timothy's teaching would more likely gain acceptance among the Jews if he were seen as one of them. It's an example of Paul's wisdom in finding ways to offset resistance to hearing the gospel message.

New Territory

By the time Paul, Silas and Timothy reached the west coast and the Roman colony of Troas (ancient Troy), they had encountered obstacles for several weeks. The account tells us that they had been "forbidden by the Holy Spirit" to speak in the Roman provinces of Bithynia and Asia, including the region known as Mysia (Acts 16:6–8). Why and exactly how this forbidding took place is unclear, but what happened next may be the key to understanding. At Troas, Paul had a dream in which he saw a Macedonian man pleading that they come over to his region. The dream was understood to be God's way of guiding their footsteps to an entirely new area for spreading the good news.

In verse 10, the writer of Acts changes his account to the first-person plural, saying, "*we* sought to go on into

Macedonia." This is apparently when Luke, the author of Acts, became part of Paul's traveling party. The narrative continues in this way till verse 17 and resumes again with "we" in chapter 20, verse 5.

Sailing the short two-day journey across the Aegean Sea from Troas to Neapolis, the men were soon on their way to Philippi in Macedonia, in what is today northern Greece. The city was given its name around 356 B.C.E. by Philip II, the father of Alexander the Great. Once the Romans conquered Macedonia in 168, they built the Egnatian Way joining the Adriatic and Aegean seas, and Philippi became a major trading and military center. Two of the assassins of Julius Caesar, Brutus and Cassius, were defeated there in 42 B.C.E. by Octavian (later Augustus Caesar) and Mark Antony. As a result, the city became a Roman colony and many veterans retired there, making its population largely Roman. The language spoken was mainly Latin, and Philippi was in some respects a miniature Rome. The way Luke describes the city has led some to wonder whether it was not his original home.

Seeking people to meet with on the Sabbath, Paul and his party went outside the city to the banks of the nearby river Gangites. There they came across a group of women who met regularly on the Sabbath for prayer. Luke writes that one of them, named Lydia, was "a worshiper of God." One translation puts it this way: "She was already a 'God-fearer'"—that is to say, she was not a Jewess but a gentile who worshiped the God of Israel. The account continues, "and the Lord opened up her heart to respond. . . ." (Acts 16:14, Jewish New Testament). This is an important point. Luke is telling us that conversion is a matter of God opening the mind to accept His way. It is not the case that we can initiate this. We cannot become converted without God acting first. According to the apostle John, Jesus said, "No one can come to me unless the Father who sent me draws him. And I will raise him up on the last day" (John 6:44).

Lydia came from the city of Thyatira in Asia Minor, a city with a Jewish community and probably the source of her knowledge of Israel's God. She was a seller of purple dye or purple cloth, for which the city was famous. The fabric was essential in the manufacture of Roman imperial clothing. This means that Lydia was very likely a woman of considerable social standing. Once her mind was opened to Paul's message, she and her household were baptized and became followers of Jesus and members of the Church of God. As a result, Paul, Silas, Luke and Timothy were invited to stay at her home for a time.

Two Kinds of Freedom

While Paul and his party were staying at Philippi, they made their way (on the Sabbath, no doubt) to the place of prayer. A young girl with fortune-telling skills followed them, calling out that they were "servants of the Most High God" who proclaimed "the way of salvation" (Acts 16:16–17). She did this for several more days, much to Paul's distress. Her masters made great profit from her abilities and were upset when Paul commanded the spirit of divination to leave her. As a result, they dragged Paul and Silas before the magistrates in the marketplace, or forum. Perhaps this was because Paul and Silas were the only full Jews in the group and therefore easier to accuse. The girl's masters told the magistrates, "These men are Jews, and they are disturbing our city. They advocate customs that are not lawful for us as Romans to accept or practice" (verses 20–21). The marketplace crowd grew angry; the magistrates tore off the two men's clothes, ordered a severe beating with rods, and threw them into the inner prison, securing their feet in the stocks.

But at midnight, as Paul and Silas were praying and singing hymns and the other prisoners listened, an earthquake shook the prison, opening all the doors and breaking the men's chains. The jailer awoke in a panic and, thinking that he had lost all the prisoners, was about to kill himself, when Paul reassured him that the prisoners were all present. The experience was enough to convince the jailer that he needed God in his life. He asked Paul and Silas what he must do, and they replied with what has become a much quoted though much misunderstood statement within traditional Christianity: "Believe in the Lord Jesus, and you will be saved, you and your household" (verse 31). Of course, there is more to it than simple belief. Believing is only the beginning. Belief is put to the test in action. It's not enough just to believe in or about Jesus; the corresponding action is to live as He lived, to let His spirit work in us as it did in Him. We have seen that a new way of life is called for once the old way has been deeply regretted and forgiven. This means that teaching of the new way is essential and must be followed. For this reason Paul would often stay in an area after people had been converted in order to teach them more about living God's way. Or he would return after a while to teach and encourage recent converts to keep on following the Way (Acts 20:1–2, 6). In this case, the jailer and his household received immediate teaching and were baptized during the night (Acts 16:32–33).

In the morning the magistrates sent word that Paul and Silas should be released quietly. But Paul insisted that the rulers come themselves, since they had beaten and imprisoned Roman citizens without cause—something forbidden in Roman society. It was the first the magistrates had heard of the men's citizenship. Fearful, they came to Paul and Silas and released them, asking them to leave the city. The two men went first to Lydia's house, visiting and encouraging the brethren before departing. Paul's later letter to the church at Philippi is one of his most encouraging. It speaks of his warm relationship with them in contrast to his treatment by the authorities (Philippians 1:3–5, 27–30). His persecution at Philippi is also verified in his first letter to the church at Thessalonica (see 1 Thessalonians 2:2), capital of the province of Macedonia—the city to which he and his group journeyed next.

Two Kinds of Listeners

Thessalonica was about 100 miles, or 160 kilometers, away. The travelers made their way there along the Egnatian Way through the ancient cities of Amphipolis and Apollonia. In 42 B.C.E. Thessalonica had been made a free city by the Romans, rather than a colony. Though it had its own form of government, the city enjoyed good relations with Rome. The emperor was held in highest esteem, and the cult of emperor worship was well established.

It is apparent from the letters Paul wrote to the church that eventually formed there that he and Silas worked very hard and met with considerable success. As usual, they went first to the synagogue. For three Sabbaths, Paul reasoned with the mixed audience (Acts 17:2). Some of the Jews were persuaded by his teaching, as were many others—described as devout Greeks, including leading women. All of these people were part of the same synagogue and worshiped the same God. Paul was able to show from the Hebrew Scriptures that the prophesied Messiah had come as Jesus of Nazareth. Thus the new congregation that formed under Paul's leadership was composed of Jews and gentiles, proselytes and God-fearers.

But once again opposition came from those Jews who were not persuaded but rather were envious of Paul's success. They raised a riot, using disreputable men from the marketplace to form a mob, unsettling the whole city. They attacked the home of one of the new converts, Jason, hoping to find Paul and his colleagues. Unable to do so, they seized Jason and some of the new brethren and dragged them before the city fathers. Then they put forward a wrongful accusation, saying that Jason had welcomed Paul and Silas who were troublemakers—men who taught that Jesus, not Caesar, was king. This stirred up the rulers and citizens, whose fear of Roman reaction brought sentence on Jason. He was to remove the visitors from his house and send them out of the city. That evening, the brethren sent Paul and his party on their way to Berea, about 45 miles (roughly 70 kilometers) to the southwest.

Berea is in the foothills of the Vérmion Mountains, a little off the beaten track today but an important town in Paul's time, prosperous and with a significant Jewish presence. There Paul spoke once more with the Jews. Luke notes that they were more fair-minded than the ones in Thessalonica (verse 11). These people were open and willing to examine the Scriptures daily, not just on the Sabbath, to see whether what Paul said was true. Soon a congregation was founded, and among them were also worshipers who were gentile in origin, men and women of high-born status.

Next Stop: Athens

Before long, Paul's Jewish opponents arrived from Thessalonica and stirred up the people once again. This time the new believers sent him on his way by sea to Athens, where he would wait for his colleagues Timothy and Silas to join him (verses 14–15).

This was Paul's only recorded visit to Athens, but it was a momentous one and the subject of a detailed section in Luke's account of early Church history.

During his time alone in the city, Paul became more and more concerned at the idolatry he saw all around. Luke writes that "his spirit was provoked within him" (verse 16). The apostle was astonished by the number of temples, altars, objects of worship, and statues of Greek gods and Roman emperors. Pausanias, the second-century traveler and geographer, wrote in his *Description of Greece* (1.24.3) that "the Athenians are far more devoted to religion than other men."

At the famous Acropolis, Paul would have seen the Parthenon and, inside, Phidias's colossal gold and ivory statue of Athena Parthenos—the "virgin Athena," goddess of the city—towering nearly 40 feet (12 meters) high. By the first century Athens had declined in importance from its classical days of greatness, and its population was probably only five or ten thousand. But it was a free city, allied with Rome, having its own form of government, and primarily an intellectual and cultural center.

All Things to All Men

As usual, Paul went first to the synagogue and reasoned with the Jewish and gentile worshipers. But in Athens he also spoke "in the marketplace every day with those who happened to be there" (verse 17). The sense is that he was willing to discuss his beliefs with anyone who wished to converse, not that he pressured people to listen. And there, just below the Acropolis, Paul came into contact not only with the general public but also with disciples of the Epicurean and Stoic schools of thought, founded by the philosophers Epicurus and Zeno.

What followed was an unusual opportunity, because most of the people Paul addressed would have held to pagan beliefs. In order to reach them, he had to use a different approach than in the synagogue. He spoke in language the Athenians could appreciate, yet he still made his point. Paul's carefully crafted words have been described by the eminent 19th-century Pauline scholars William J. Conybeare and John S. Howson as "full of the most impressive teaching for every age of the world." These authors concluded, "We cannot fail to notice how the sentences of this interrupted speech are constructed to meet the cases in succession of every class of which the audience was composed."

For the Stoics, the divine was everywhere and in everything. They were pantheists who believed that at death the human spirit returns to God for fiery "recycling"; in that sense, for them, there was no personal afterlife. Further, they said that everything that happens is God's will and should not be resisted. Their code was an austere one of both self-denial and apathy. The Epicureans, on the other hand, were as close to being atheists as people who still made reference to the gods could be. They held that death was final, that everything happened by chance, and that the gods were of shadowy substance, remote and disinterested at best in humanity, and therefore life should be spent in pursuit of the highest form of pleasure—the removal of all pain.

According to Luke, the Athenians in general were known for spending their time in passing around the latest news and ideas. Much of the discussion took place in the Stoa, or colonnaded area, around the marketplace.

As Paul addressed the crowd, the reaction to his words about Jesus and the resurrection was mostly negative. Some of the philosophers tossed ideas back and forth with him and eventually insulted him, referring to him as an ignorant show-off. The offending word in Greek meant, literally, "a seed picker," a lazy person who made a living from picking up scraps of food. In Paul's case, the term referred not to food but to bits of religious or philosophical knowledge, and thus to a person who spoke without real knowledge. Others in the audience were concerned that Paul was breaking an Athenian law against the introduction of new gods. Inviting him to explain his ideas further, they took him either to nearby Mars Hill (if that was still the meeting place of the Areopagus, or official court of the government of Athens) or to a place within the Stoa (verses 18–21).

Paul's discourse was masterful. He said that during his stay he had noticed that the Athenians were "very religious," because they worshiped many objects. Though Paul was in fact greatly distressed by the city's open idolatry, his language remained courteous and friendly. He said that he had come upon an altar dedicated to "the unknown god." (That such altars existed in Athens is supported by Pausanias's mention of them about a hundred years after Paul was there.) Thus Paul could not be convicted of introducing a new god, since he claimed that their unknown god was the very God he represented, and that they worshiped Him without realizing it.

Then, on the basis of the good will he had created, Paul made an audacious comment. Surrounded by the area's many temples, he said, "The God who made the world and everything in it, being Lord of heaven and earth, does not live in temples made by man." Further, he said, the God he was speaking of could not be "served by human hands, as though he needed anything, since he himself gives to all mankind life and breath and everything" (verses 24–25). Here Paul seemed to be alluding first to the Greek dramatist Euripides, who wrote, "God, if he be truly God, has need of nothing" and second, to Seneca, who wrote that "God seeks no servants . . . he himself serves mankind."

Paul continued to explain that God had "made from one man every nation of mankind to live on all the face of the earth, having determined allotted periods and the boundaries of their dwelling place." The apostle had no intention of talking only about the God of ancient Israel but about the God of all humanity. This common origin of mankind was not a truth that the Athenians would have appreciated, believing as they did that they were a unique people. But Paul noted that this common ancestry meant that all humanity "should seek God, in the hope that they might feel their way toward him and find him. Yet he is actually not far from each one of us" (verses 26–27). Paul had his doubts that the Athenians *would* seek Him, but certainly God intended that they should.

Next he said, "For 'in him we live and move and have our being'; as even some of your own poets have said." Many scholars believe that here Paul quoted Epimenides of Crete, who, according to legend, went around erecting altars to anonymous gods. In one of his poems, addressing the supreme god, he wrote: "They fashioned a tomb for thee, O holy and high one—the Cretans, always liars, evil beasts, idle bellies! But thou art not dead: thou livest and abidest forever, for in thee we live and move and have our being." Extending the argument, Paul said, "For we are indeed his offspring." This is yet another quote, this time from the poem *Phenomena* by Aratus of Cilicia. Cilicia was, of course, Paul's birthplace, and this perhaps accounts for his familiarity with the poet's work.

Paul's main argument was that the worship of idols has nothing to do with the one true God who created everything. Thus he was saying that idolatry is wrong, because nothing that man can fashion can even approximate the Creator and certainly should not be worshiped. What was needed was for the Athenians to change their evil ways, to turn around and to go the other way. Further, he said, because the world has sinned in many ways, idolatry being just one of them, God will send a man to judge the world. Then, startlingly, he said that the man God will send has already been resurrected from the dead.

At the mention of the resurrection, some made fun of Paul, some said they would like to hear more later, and some believed him (verse 32). Among the latter was a leader of the Areopagus, Dionysius. Members of this court were chosen from among the archons, or leaders of the city, which gives us a clue to Dionysius's status in Athenian society. From Paul's unique approach to delivering the message came additional believers: a woman named Damaris and several others.

Nothing more is known of the Athenian church, but the manner in which Paul addressed this unusual audience confirms that he tried, as he said in one of his letters, to be "all things to all people" (1 Corinthians 9:22).

On to Corinth

From Athens, Paul traveled 50 miles (80 kilometers) to the west to the commercial capital of the area, Corinth. The classical city seems to have been established in the eighth or ninth century B.C.E. and was almost completely destroyed by the Romans in 146 B.C.E. A century later, Julius Caesar recreated it as a Roman colony, populating it with freedmen. By the 50s C.E., when Paul went there, it was once again becoming the wealthiest city in southern Greece.

Like most cities with port facilities, Corinth fostered a mobile and decadent society. But its everyday moral problems were only made worse by local religious practices. Early in the first century C.E., the geographer Strabo claimed that a thousand female slave prostitutes, having been dedicated as offerings, had at one time been active at the Temple of Aphrodite. While that is disputed, it is known that the temple, which was associated with immorality, was restored in Roman times. In this challenging and corrupt environment, Paul stayed for 18 months (Acts 18:11) and established a group of followers of the Way. It was here, too, that he began to write some of the letters that form a major part of the New Testament. The first were his two letters to the church he had helped form a few months earlier at Thessalonica.

When Paul arrived in Corinth, he met two Jews, Aquila and his wife, Priscilla, who had recently been expelled from Rome under an imperial decree promulgated by Claudius Caesar in about 49 C.E. The Roman biographer Suetonius records that Claudius drove the Jews out of the capital because they were causing trouble at the prompting of one "Chrestus." Whether this was an individual's name or an inaccurate spelling of "Christus" is not known. That Jews were persecuted by three successive emperors of the period is well established. It is not surprising that as Jews under persecution, Aquila and Priscilla went to Corinth; it was a crossroads of the ancient world and had a Jewish community. There Paul stayed with the couple, since they shared the same occupation: tent-making and leatherwork.

Near the forum in Corinth, on the Lechaion Road, archaeologists have found part of an inscription on white marble. It is thought to have read in full "Synagogue of the Hebrews" and would have been placed over the door of the meeting place. It confirms that there were enough Jews in Corinth in the period to warrant such a building. In fact, the New Testament mentions the presence of a synagogue at the time of Paul's visit. Luke tells us that Paul went there every Sabbath and spoke with Jews and gentiles, proselytes and God-fearers.

When Silas and Timothy arrived from Macedonia, Paul devoted his whole time to speaking and left off working with Aquila and Priscilla. Unfortunately, most of the Jews and proselytes rejected the message, and Paul decided to deal solely with the gentiles. Only a few from the synagogue immediately became members of the Church. First was Titius Justus, who lived by the synagogue and was a God-fearer. And, surprising to the Jews, the others were the synagogue ruler, Crispus, and his household. As a result, other Corinthians soon joined the group. Paul confirms in his first letter to the Corinthian church that he personally baptized Crispus, and Luke records in Acts that many others were baptized (Acts 18:5–8; 1 Corinthians 1:14).

Paul was able to continue teaching from the safety of Justus's house until opposition boiled over once more. When Corinth received its newly appointed Roman proconsul, Gallio, in 51 C.E., some of the Jews seized the opportunity to complain to him about Paul. Gallio was an older brother of the Roman philosopher Seneca, who later became an advisor to Emperor Nero. Despite the fact that Crispus, a man of influence, had become a follower of the Way, Paul was accused of persuading people to worship God against the law. In effect, his opponents said that he was promoting an illegal religion. It was a weak argument. Paul was a Jew, and Judaism was a legally recognized religion in the Roman Empire. Gallio quickly saw the case against Paul as an internal Jewish matter and threw it out of court, effectively recognizing the followers of Jesus as a legal part of Judaism. This ruling allowed the Corinthian church to flourish (Acts 18:12–16).

What kind of teaching did Paul bring to the Church members in Corinth during his long stay there? Did he launch a new religion, as his accusers claimed and as many claim today? Was Paul the founder of a new religion or a follower of Jesus? His two extant letters to the congregation at Corinth tell us in detail what he taught. Take the following statement, for example: "I received from the Lord what I also delivered to you, that the Lord Jesus on the night when he was betrayed took bread, and when he had given thanks, he broke it, and said, 'This is my body which is for you. Do this in remembrance of me.' In the same way also he took the cup, after supper, saying, 'This cup is the new covenant in my blood. Do this, as often as you drink it, in remembrance of me.' For as often as you eat this bread and drink the cup, you proclaim the Lord's death until he comes" (1 Corinthians 11:23–26).

Here, in a brief passage, we see that Paul followed his Master exactly. In this case, he taught and practiced what Jesus did on His final Passover evening with His disciples. And this letter was written 20 years after Paul became a follower. But did he recommend that followers emulate Jesus in other ways? For example, did he expect them to keep the Sabbath and holy days just as the Jews of that time did, and as Jesus Himself had done? In 1 Corinthians, Paul writes to Jews and gentiles that he expects them to keep a feast that the ancient Israelites had kept: "Cleanse out the old leaven that you may be a new lump, as you really are unleavened. For Christ, our Passover lamb, has been sacrificed. Let us therefore celebrate the festival, not with the old leaven, the leaven of malice and evil, but with the unleavened bread of sincerity and truth" (1 Corinthians 5:7–8). When he speaks of keeping or observing "the festival," he is speaking of the Feast of the Passover and the Days of Unleavened Bread, something that Jesus Himself kept (see Luke 22:1, 7–8). Even in the gentile world, Paul was following Jesus' example down to the letter by teaching and observing the holy days that God had commanded ancient Israel to keep.

After many months, Paul determined to return to Antioch in Syria; by the time he left Corinth, he had spent at least a year and a half teaching and establishing the new community of believers there (Acts 18:11). On the first leg of his journey back to Antioch, the husband-and-wife tent-making team, fellow believers Aquila and Priscilla, accompanied him. They departed by ship from Corinth's eastern port of Cenchrea, sailing eastward across the Aegean to Ephesus, the capital of the Roman province of Asia and home to the governor. The port city was known as "the Treasure House of Asia" for its preeminence in the province's trade.

As we will see, Paul ended up spending a considerable length of time in Ephesus.

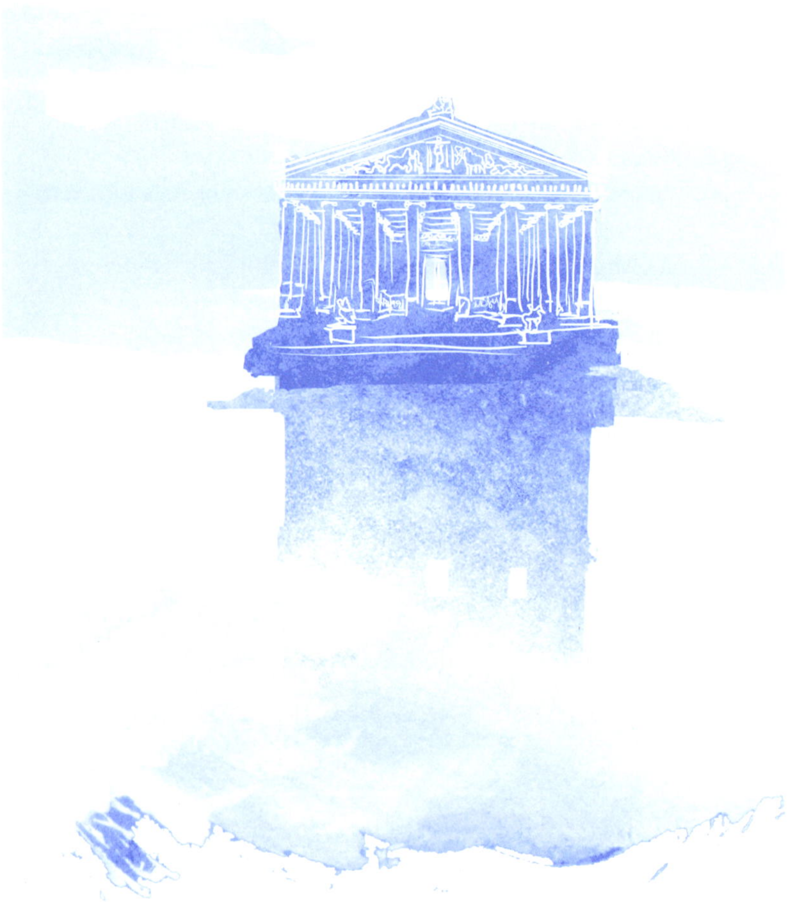

Chapter Four

From Ephesus to Jerusalem

Ephesus was known throughout the Roman Empire as the site of one of the seven wonders of the ancient world, the much-visited Temple of Artemis.

When Paul arrived at Ephesus, his appearance was a little different than it had been at the end of his stay in Corinth. Just before leaving Cenchrea, he had cut his hair short to mark the completion of a vow he had made (verse 18). Though the book of Acts makes no comment about the reason for Paul's vow, it was likely in accord with instructions given in the Hebrew Scriptures. If Israelite men or women wished to make a vow in dedication to serving God in a particular way for up to 30 days, they temporarily became "Nazirites" (from the Hebrew *nazir,* "consecrated"). During the period of the vow, they consumed no grape product nor strong drink, did not cut their hair, and avoided contact with dead bodies.

Once the self-imposed restrictions were over, Nazirites were to purify themselves and shave their heads, typically at the central place of worship: in earlier times the "tent of meeting" (Numbers 6:18), or later, the temple in Jerusalem. When they were too far from the temple, they had to modify that practice somewhat. Thus Paul, who was traveling among the Diaspora at the time, could only cut his hair short to signify the completing of his vow. The vow seems to have been related to his time in Corinth and perhaps to his gratitude for God's continued help there. This episode, as recorded by Luke, shows that Paul was not opposed to living according to the ceremonial law of the God of ancient Israel.

When the ship docked in Ephesus, Paul took his leave of Priscilla and Aquila and went to the local synagogue as usual to reason with the congregation. His discourse was intriguing enough to cause the listeners to ask him to stay on, but he was intent on returning to his home area after a visit to Jerusalem. Promising to return if possible, he set sail for Caesarea, the capital of Roman Palestine. After traveling up to Jerusalem to greet the church (a mark of his close relationship and respect for the brethren and leaders there), he went on to Antioch. Then, after some time there, he started out on another extensive journey to the region we know as Asia Minor (verses 19–23).

Teaching and Ministering

During Paul's absence, a Jew named Apollos from the Egyptian city of Alexandria had arrived in Ephesus. He began to preach in the synagogue about Jesus and His message. Apollos was familiar with John the Baptist's call to repentance, and although he had knowledge of Jesus, he did not know about the need for the believer to be transformed by the Holy Spirit. Priscilla and Aquila heard him, and recognizing that there were gaps in his knowledge, they took him aside and helped him understand what was missing in his public addresses. Apollos then went on to Corinth with the encouragement and support of the Ephesian brethren and spoke openly and boldly to the Jews there (verses 24–28).

At this point Paul was approaching Ephesus from the inland provinces of Galatia and Phrygia, where he had been encouraging the communities established on his previous journeys. When he arrived in the city, he met some believers—about 12 in all—influenced perhaps by Apollos's teachings. In response to Paul's questions about the process of their conversion, they said that they had not even heard of the Holy Spirit. Like Priscilla and Aquila before him, Paul found himself explaining that belief in Jesus meant not only baptism by immersion in water but also receipt of the

Holy Spirit (Acts 19:1–7). The willingness of the group to be rebaptized signified their humility and led to their receiving the gift of God through the agency of Paul, who laid his hands on them in prayer.

Soon after, Paul kept his promise to the Ephesian Jews and returned to teaching in the local synagogue for about three months. His reasoning was convincing to some and persuaded them of the truth about God's coming kingdom on the earth. It was only when others in the synagogue rejected what he had to say and spoke critically of the Way (of life) he represented that he started teaching his disciples and others each day in a local lecture hall belonging to Tyrannus, a teacher or philosopher. It's possible that Paul taught during the heat of the day, between 11 a.m. and 4 p.m., when the school was not in use. This schedule would have allowed him to also work for his living, as he noted to the Ephesians (Acts 20:34).

Once at the school, he met with much success. Luke tells us that "this continued for two years, so that all the residents of Asia heard the word of the Lord, both Jews and Greeks" (Acts 19:10). Paul's time in Ephesus was the longest he spent anywhere (a later note tells us that he stayed for three years; see 20:31). Though most of the Jewish community rejected his message, some did believe. But Paul's greatest success came among the God-fearing non-Jewish population in the city and the surrounding area.

One of the remarkable aspects of Paul's time in Ephesus was God's healing of various illnesses. In some cases, just a headband or apron that had touched Paul had a restorative effect on the sick and those possessed of evil spirits (Acts 19:11–12). This power impressed some wandering Jewish exorcists, who appropriated the name of Jesus in an attempt to cast out evil spirits. But they were unable to bring about the same positive effect as Paul since they were not genuine believers. In fact, seven of the exorcists, who were sons of a Jewish high priest named Sceva, were overpowered and injured by a possessed man whom they tried to heal.

The news of this episode spread around Ephesus, making the name and power of Jesus very well known among all the community. So convicted were those who became believers that they brought their books of magic, valued at 50,000 silver coins, and burned them publicly (verses 17-20). This dramatic reversal also worked in favor of Paul's ministry, because the city was a center of healing superstitions and charlatans who claimed recuperative powers.

It is reasonable to suggest that at this point Paul made a second visit to Corinth, and that after returning to Ephesus he wrote a now lost letter (see 1 Corinthians 5:9) as well as the one we know as 1 Corinthians (see 1 Corinthians 16:8, 19). Luke tells us in Acts 19:21 that in Ephesus Paul also began making plans to visit Macedonia, Greece, Jerusalem and Rome. He refers to this intended visit in 1 Corinthians 16:5, proposing to make yet a third visit to Corinth. Paul's first step was to send two of his helpers, Timothy and Erastus, ahead to Macedonia. From there Timothy was to go on to Corinth (1 Corinthians 4:17; 16:10-11). Meanwhile Paul stayed in Ephesus (see also 1 Corinthians 16:8-9), but only until events overtook him and he was forced to leave.

Artemis, Artisans and the Amphitheater

Ephesus was known throughout the Roman Empire as the site of one of the seven wonders of the ancient world, the much-visited Temple of Artemis. Paul would have seen the temple as his ship entered the estuary of the River Cayster and approached its harbor, which had been specially dredged to accommodate sea traffic. Just to the north beyond the dock stood the massive edifice—more than 400 feet long by 200 feet wide (120 meters by 60 meters)—with its 127 marble columns, each nearly 60 feet, or 18 meters, tall. Inside stood a statue of the fertility goddess, Artemis of the Ephesians, possibly carved from a black meteorite (significant to the inhabitants because it had fallen from the sky and was presumed to be a gift of the gods). The idol's temple, which was four times the size of the Parthenon in Athens, also served as a central bank and as a sanctuary for those accused of criminal activity.

The other major structure visible from the harbor was the amphitheater, still intact today and seating about 25,000. This was the site of the riot that precipitated Paul's sudden departure. Local craftsmen had been making a living from the manufacture of small silver shrines to Artemis. One of them, the silversmith Demetrius, accused Paul and his colleagues of subverting their business by teaching the people that gods made by human hands were worthless idols. Sensing that this would ruin their business and shame the city, which was an official protector of the cult of Artemis, the tradesmen became enraged and dragged two of Paul's Macedonian companions, Gaius and Aristarchus, into the amphitheater. In the confusion that ensued, Paul wanted to follow them in and address the crowd. But his supporters, including not only Church members but also several Asiarchs ("rulers of Asia," or city leaders), begged him not to do so (verses 23–32).

The crowd would not even allow a local Jew named Alexander to make a defense but shouted him down for two hours as they chanted, "Great is Artemis of the Ephesians!" The city's chief executive, or "town clerk," finally restored order and addressed them. He pointed out that everyone knew "that the city of the Ephesians is temple keeper of the great Artemis, and of the sacred stone that fell from the sky" (verses 33–35). Thus there could be no danger from men who had not in fact blasphemed the goddess. And after all, there were courts where any such accusation could be lodged. He advised all to go home lest the Roman authorities call them into question for the uproar. This was the opportune moment for Paul to depart the city.

Observing Holy Days

What followed was about a year of visiting the Macedonian churches (during which time Paul wrote 2 Corinthians and referred to his previous difficult visit to their city; see 2 Corinthians 2:1 and 13:2), a possible stop in Illyricum (a Roman province on the eastern shore of the Adriatic; see Romans 15:19), and a three-month stay with the followers in Greece. He then started his homeward journey.

Escaping a plot against him by the Jews in Greece, he traveled circuitously through Macedonia instead of directly to Syria as originally planned. There he and Luke stopped for a few days in Philippi. Meanwhile, their seven traveling companions went ahead and waited for them at Troas (Troy) on the eastern side of the Aegean, where there were also Church members. Giving an important clue to early Church practice, Luke notes that he and Paul left Philippi "after the Days of Unleavened Bread" (Acts 20:6). This is not merely a calendar reference; it again conveys that Paul continued to observe the holy days prescribed in the Torah (see Leviticus 23). As we have seen, the members at Philippi were of gentile and/or proselyte background. Yet as converts, with their teacher among them, they would have kept the Passover and the Days of Unleavened Bread, albeit with new significance after the coming of Jesus Christ (1 Corinthians 5:7–8).

Joining his companions in Troas after a five-day sea journey, Paul spent the next week there. On a Saturday evening as they prepared for a final meal with the local church, he gave a lengthy address, speaking till midnight. A young man sitting on a third-floor window sill fell asleep and tumbled to the ground. Though he was presumed dead, Paul reassured everyone and took him into his arms; to everyone's great joy, the youth was alive.

After a meal, the apostle continued speaking till daybreak, when he and his party went on their way. Paul walked overland that day and met his companions a little way south at Assos, where they had arrived by ship. Together they sailed past Ephesus and landed at the next main port, Miletus. Paul had determined not to stop at Ephesus because he was hurrying to be in Jerusalem by Pentecost (Acts 20:7–16). And here is another important reference to Paul's observance of God's prescribed holy days.

From Miletus, he called for the Ephesian church elders to travel the 30 or so miles (about 50 kilometers) overland to meet him. When they arrived, Paul took the opportunity to deliver a heart-to-heart talk about his ministry among them, and a warning about what would come to the church in their care if human ambition got in their way. He began by reminding them of his own example of hard work and humility from the start of his service among them. He had taught both publicly and privately—the preaching and teaching aspects of his work as a minister. He had explained to Jews and gentiles alike the need for repentance before God of sinful ways, and for faith in Jesus Christ's paying the death penalty for that sin, so that forgiveness could come from God.

Paul was taking his leave of them and going to Jerusalem, fully aware that he might never see them again, because through the Holy Spirit he was becoming convinced wherever he traveled that he was destined for imprisonment and physical suffering (verses 22–23). His only concern was that he would be able to complete the work God had given him.

Then Paul reminded the elders of their duty to care for "the church of God." He foresaw that there would be attacks on the membership from outside—from, as he put it, "fierce wolves." And some of the elders, he warned, would succumb to the temptation to draw away disciples for themselves, teaching false doctrine. It was a sobering message, concluded with a reminder of his example of hard work to help the weak, and of living by Jesus' words, "It is more blessed to give than to receive" (verses 28–35).

In parting, Paul knelt down and prayed with the tearful men, who sorrowed that he had said they would see him no more.

Bound for Troubles

Boarding a ship bound for Tyre, Paul and his party left Asia behind. When they arrived in the ancient Phoenician city, they disembarked and spent a week with believers there. Following a one-day stop with the Church members in Ptolemais, they went on to Caesarea, where "for many days" they were guests of Philip the evangelist, one of the original seven deacons at Jerusalem (see Acts 6), and his four daughters. When a prophet named Agabus arrived from Judea, it was to warn Paul that in Jerusalem he would be bound and delivered to a foreign power. Though his companions and the members in Caesarea begged him not to go, Paul couldn't be deterred. Accompanied by some of the members, he and his companions arrived in Jerusalem, where an early disciple, Mnason of Cyprus, gave them lodging (Acts 21:1–16).

Welcomed warmly by the Jerusalem brethren, Paul went the next day to visit James, the brother of Jesus, and the other elders. He related the success of the work among gentiles in the Diaspora, at which news they were delighted. They expressed one concern, however, and gave him a way to offset the reputation he had developed among some of the believing Jews. It seems he was wrongly thought to have been teaching Jews against the law delivered by Moses regarding infant circumcision and the ancient Israelite customs. The elders therefore advised him to ritually purify himself, to go to the temple with four believers who were about to complete a vow, and to pay their expenses so that at the end of seven days they could have their heads shaven. This would be proof to all that Paul did honor the law. The elders mentioned again that they were in agreement with him about what the gentiles should do in respect of becoming members of the community of believers (see Acts 15), and they spoke of the letter they had sent with Paul to the church in Antioch, in which they confirmed that adult male circumcision was not required of gentile converts (Acts 21:17–25).

Their proposal for clearing Paul's name was well intentioned, and Paul complied with the elders' request, but just before his week of purification was ended, he was accosted in the temple—not by fellow believers but by some nonbelieving Jews from Asia, no doubt also in Jerusalem for the Feast of Pentecost. His attackers, probably from Ephesus, pointed him out as "the man who is teaching everyone everywhere against the people and the law and this place" (verse 28). They further accused him of defiling the temple by bringing gentiles into the part reserved for Jewish worshipers. It was a false accusation, as they had merely seen him in the city with one of his companions, Trophimus, a gentile from Ephesus.

The ensuing riot brought the Roman garrison guard of soldiers and centurions, as well as Claudius Lysias, their commander or tribune, to the scene. Their arrival stopped Paul's beating at the hands of the mob that had by now dragged him into the Court of the Gentiles, the temple gates being closed to prevent Paul gaining sanctuary and to make sure the sacred area wouldn't be defiled by murder.

The tribune arrested and chained Paul and tried to ascertain what had happened, but the crowd was so wild and noisy that it was impossible to get the story straight. Paul was escorted to the barracks, probably in the adjacent Antonia fortress, and carried up the steps by the soldiers for his own protection from the crowd still shouting out for his death. On the steps, he asked Claudius Lysias, in Greek, if he could address the crowd. The tribune agreed, surprised that the prisoner could speak the language: he had assumed that Paul was the wanted Egyptian leader of 4,000 terrorists, or *sicarii* (assassins). This same Egyptian is mentioned by the Jewish historian Josephus as being active during the rule of Felix, the Roman procurator of Palestine (52–60 C.E.), before whom Paul would soon appear. Paul answered the tribune that, to the contrary, he was a Jewish citizen of Tarsus in Cilicia, well known as a Hellenic educational center (verses 37–39).

A Deft Defense

With permission to speak, Paul motioned with his hand and the crowd quieted. What follows is another example of his ability to communicate with an audience effectively and economically. Having spoken to great effect in Greek to the commander moments earlier, he now turned to the murderous mob and addressed them politely in a Hebrew dialect, Aramaic. He began in a way designed to elicit their attention: "Brothers and fathers [or "My companions and my elders"], listen while I explain why I am not guilty" (Acts 22:1, paraphrased). Luke's account says that "when they heard that he was addressing them in the Hebrew language, they became even more quiet" (verse 2).

Paul then told his story, crafted in such a way as to keep his audience attentive. He gave them reason to identify with him further, relating that he was an Israelite, born in the Diaspora city of Tarsus, but educated in Jerusalem by a famous teacher, Gamaliel, in the Pharisaic school of thought. He was zealous for God "as all of you are this day." In effect, "I am just like you." He related how he had persecuted the followers of Jesus ("this Way") to the death, the high priest and the council of Jewish leaders, the Sanhedrin, being his witnesses; it was from them that he had gained approval to go to Damascus to take Jesus' disciples captive and bring them to Jerusalem for punishment. In other words, "I was as opposed to the sect as you now are to me."

Then, making the turn in his argument, he began to give account of his change of heart. He explained what had happened to him on the road to Damascus, how he had been temporarily blinded and how he had become a follower of the Way. He showed how a devout and well-respected Jew had been God's intermediary to restore his sight and had delivered a message from Him. He explained that it was even *in the temple,* as he prayed, that Jesus had revealed to him in vision that he was to leave Jerusalem, where his message would be opposed. Paul then showed how he had argued that the Jerusalemites would surely listen because he had participated in the persecution of Jesus' followers, including the martyr Stephen (see Acts 7:57–8:3). But Jesus had told him, "Go, for I will send you far away to the Gentiles" (Acts 22:21).

It was the word *Gentiles* that ended Paul's speech. Despite all of his rhetorical skill, the crowd was now on fire again. It was all they had to hear to erupt into another riot and demand his death.

At this, the tribune took Paul inside the barracks to "examine" him by flogging, in the hope of finding out why he was the cause of such uproar. He had likely not understood the prisoner's defense, given in Aramaic. All he could see was the result.

At the prospect of severe punishment, Paul's presence of mind helped him once more as it had in Philippi. As the soldiers stretched him out for the whipping, he asked a centurion whether it was lawful to flog an uncondemned Roman citizen. Of course it was not, and Paul knew it. When the tribune learned of Paul's question, he came immediately and questioned him about his citizenship, admitting that his own had been purchased. Paul replied that he was Roman by birth—a superior form of citizenship. Now the soldiers and their leader were afraid. The next day, Claudius Lysias had Paul freed from his chains and brought him together with the chief priests and the Sanhedrin to ask more about the reasons for the riot (verses 25–30).

Paul's opening remarks were similar to those made to the crowd. Addressing them as "brothers," he said that he had always lived in good conscience before God. At that, Ananias, the high priest (47–58 C.E.), told those next to him to hit him in the mouth. Paul's anger flared: "God is going to strike you, you whitewashed wall!" He was incensed at such hypocrisy and injustice coming from one who as a judge was ignoring the very law he was representing. This caused further alienation for Paul, who had not realized that he was addressing the high priest himself. He quickly apologized, knowing that the Scriptures said, "You shall not speak evil of a ruler of your people" (Acts 23:1–5; see also Exodus 22:28).

But how was Paul to get back control of the situation with his opponents? Knowing that some were Sadducees and some were Pharisees, he exploited a crucial difference in their beliefs and spoke the truth at the same time. The Sadducees did not accept the existence of angels or spirits or that the dead will be resurrected. Paul said loudly, "Brothers, I am a Pharisee, a son of Pharisees. It is with respect to the hope and the resurrection of the dead that I am on trial" (verse 6). This brought the meeting to an impasse, with each side noisily arguing its perspective, some of the Pharisees now protesting strongly and supporting Paul: "We find nothing wrong in this man. What if a spirit or an angel spoke to him?" (verse 9). When the situation turned violent and Paul's life was again in danger from the contending parties, the tribune intervened and had him taken back to the barracks.

That night Paul was encouraged by Jesus, who appeared before him and told him, "As you have testified to the facts about me in Jerusalem, so you must testify also in Rome" (verse 11).

On to Felix

The next day more than 40 Jews conspired together to kill Paul and bound themselves by an oath not to eat or drink until they had succeeded. That's to say, the threat was immediate. The 40 zealots went to the elders and priests and told them to ask the tribune to send the prisoner to them for further questioning, whereupon the conspirators would kill him. But Paul's nephew heard of the plot and informed his uncle. Paul called one of the officers, who took the young man to Claudius Lysias. Once the tribune understood what was about to take place, he told the nephew to say nothing more about it, and he arranged for Paul to have a couple of horses and an escort of 470 soldiers to accompany him by night to the coastal fortress of Caesarea. There he would be judged by Felix the governor, who, according to the letter the tribune wrote, should hear the council's case against the Roman citizen once more, even though Claudius Lysias had found nothing worthy of death in Paul's behavior (verses 12–30).

On arrival, Felix asked Paul where he was from and, hearing that it was Cilicia, put him in the palace built by Herod the Great until his accusers should come.

Presenting legal cases to Roman authorities demanded certain skills, and the Jewish leaders decided that their best chance for success was to use a professional orator and lawyer named Tertullus. When he arrived five days later with Ananias and some of his elders, he was primed: "Since through you we enjoy much peace, and since by your foresight, most excellent Felix, reforms are being made for this nation, in every way and everywhere we accept this with all gratitude" (Acts 24:1–3). His generous opening soon gave way to three religiously based accusations, supported by the Jews. Paul, he said, was a dangerous nuisance, a man who started riots among the Jews everywhere and a leader of a religious party, or sect, identified as the Nazarenes. His hope was that Felix would see Paul as a political nuisance, a threat to public order.

The governor motioned for Paul to speak. The apostle also began with a compliment to Felix, mentioning his long years of service as a judge to the nation. Paul welcomed his knowledgeable oversight. Inviting the governor to ascertain that it was only 12 days since he had gone up to Jerusalem, he said that even during that short time there had been no evidence of his causing problems in synagogues or the temple. The accusations were false and his opponents had no proof.

Paul was willing to admit one thing, however—that he was a follower of the Way that his detractors had derogatorily called a sect. The Way, he said, was consistent with the law and the prophets. Further, he said his enemies believed in the resurrection as he did. The purpose of his visit to Jerusalem was to bring a charitable gift to his nation and to present offerings at the temple. As he was doing so, Ephesian

Jews had wrongfully accused him and started a riot. And as his present accusers well knew, he was now standing before Felix only because he had called out among them, "It is with respect to the resurrection of the dead that I am on trial before you this day" (verses 14–21).

Felix, whom Luke tells us had "a rather accurate knowledge of the Way" (his wife Drusilla being Jewish), put off the hearing, saying that he wanted Claudius Lysias to attend a future meeting before making a decision. Paul was allowed to remain under relatively open house arrest, with his friends able to visit and help him.

Another Governor, Another Hearing

After a few days, Felix sent for Paul and listened as he explained about having faith in Jesus Christ. The governor became frightened when Paul talked further about "righteousness and self-control and the coming judgment" (verse 25), telling him that he would talk to him again later. Luke notes that Felix was hoping for a bribe and so kept sending for him. This went on for two years until Felix was replaced by Porcius Festus. But because Felix wanted to do the Jews a parting favor, he left Paul in prison.

When Festus had been in the province just three days, he went up to Jerusalem from Caesarea. Ever eager to get rid of Paul, the religious leaders urged the new governor to send him back to Jerusalem, planning to ambush and kill him on the way. Festus would only agree to try the case in the provincial capital and asked that the Jewish leaders send a delegation there. After about 10 days he went back to Caesarea and the next day asked that Paul be brought before him, the Jerusalem leaders being present.

As before, accusations flew, but the argument seemed to Festus to be about matters of the Jewish religion and someone called Jesus, who had died (yet who Paul said was alive), rather than a serious crime (Acts 25:1–7; see also verses 18–19).

Paul argued in his own defense, "Neither against the law of the Jews, nor against the temple, nor against Caesar have I committed any offense" (verse 8). In an attempt to please the religious leaders, Festus asked Paul if he would go back to Jerusalem to be tried before him. Now Paul replied more forcefully. Pleasing the Jews was insufficient reason to try him in Jerusalem. Since he had done nothing against the law, the temple or the emperor, he exercised his right of appeal as a Roman citizen to stand before Caesar himself and be heard. Festus first consulted with his advisors, then granted Paul's request: "To Caesar you have appealed; to Caesar you shall go" (verse 12). Yet Festus knew that he did not have enough information on the nature of the charge against Paul to send him immediately to Rome (see verse 27).

After some time, the local king, Herod Agrippa II, arrived in Caesarea with his sister Bernice to pay respects to the new governor. Though Agrippa ruled a small area north of Palestine, he had the authority to appoint the Jewish chief priest. Festus took the opportunity to mention Paul to Agrippa, hoping perhaps for some guidance in what he might tell Caesar about the prisoner. The next day Paul had his audience with the king. Agrippa, Bernice and their entourage entered Herod's palace with great pomp. High-ranking military men and city fathers were there as Paul was brought in. In explaining the prisoner's situation, Festus recapped his previous judgment: "I found that he had done nothing deserving death" (verse 25). Agrippa then said to Paul, "You have permission to speak for yourself."

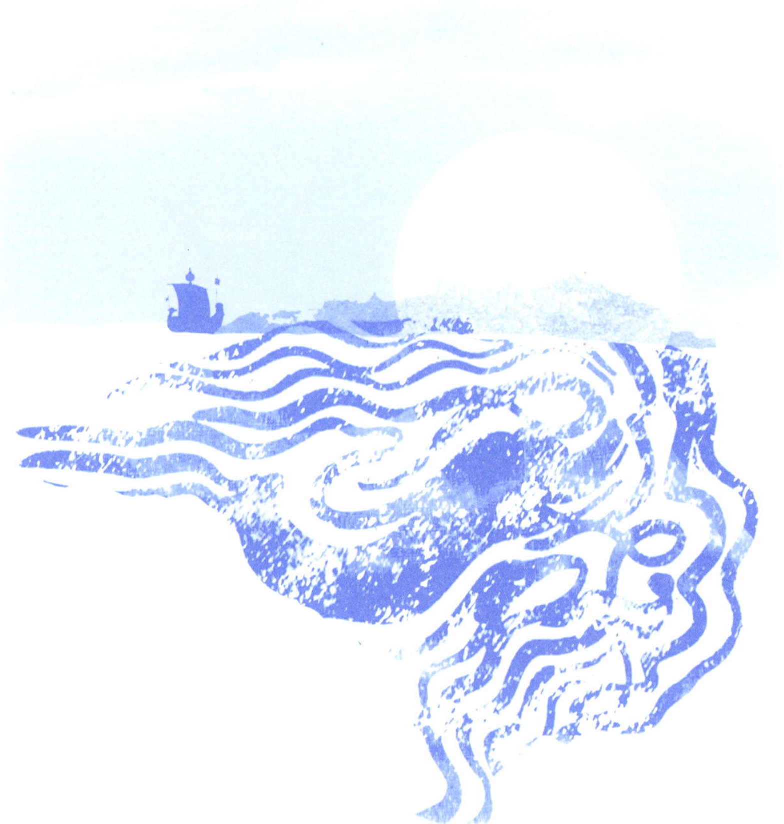

Chapter Five

On to Rome

Luke writes in great detail about the journey, demonstrating technical knowledge of travel by sea in those times. There is an authenticity in his record, supporting his claim to have been an eyewitness to much of Paul's ministry.

Paul began his defense before Agrippa by noting the king's familiarity with Jewish customs and controversies, and said that he felt fortunate to be addressing such a well-informed man. He then outlined his history as a Pharisee and their common belief in the resurrection of the dead. Yet that very belief was the reason for his arrest. He mentioned his persecution of the early Church, authorized by the high priest, and his life-changing experience on the road to Damascus, when Jesus appeared to him. His received commission from that point on was to teach the gentiles Jesus' message. Paul invited Agrippa to understand how impossible it was for him to do other than proclaim what Jesus had commanded—that people should turn to God and change their lives. Jesus had died but was now alive as the savior of "our people and . . . the Gentiles" (Acts 26:1–23).

At this point Festus interrupted, saying that Paul was out of his mind, that his extensive learning had made him mad. No, said Paul, "I am speaking true and rational words." What is more, "the king knows about these things," because "this has not been done in a corner" (verses 24–26). Focusing directly on the monarch, Paul asked him boldly, "King Agrippa, do you believe the prophets? I know that you believe."

Agrippa's reply was in the form of a cynical question: "Are you trying to quickly make a Christian out of me?" (verse 28, paraphrased). Paul replied that he wished everyone could be as he was, except for the chains.

At this, Agrippa, his sister Bernice and their entourage got up and left, admitting to each other later that Paul had done nothing worthy of death or imprisonment. In fact, were it not that he had appealed to Caesar, he could have been released, said the king. But the die had been cast. He would have to go to Rome.

At Sea Again

Released to Julius, a centurion of the Emperor's Regiment, Paul and his companions boarded a ship for Italy along with other prisoners. But he had no way of knowing the difficulties ahead. It would be a lengthy voyage with several ports of call. Luke writes in great detail about the journey, demonstrating technical knowledge of travel by sea in those times. There is an authenticity in his record, supporting his claim to have been an eyewitness to much of Paul's ministry. The apostle's other companion on this journey was Aristarchus of Thessalonica, in Macedonia (Acts 27:2).

The ship's first stop was at Sidon, where Paul was allowed to disembark and meet with members of the Church. The voyage then continued safely along the northeast coast of Cyprus despite contrary winds, and across the open sea to the coast of Cilicia, Pamphylia and Lycia. There at the port of Myra the party changed ships. Again because of adverse winds, they sailed slowly westward past Rhodes and Cnidus to the leeward side of Crete. They came to one of the island's harbors, Fair Havens, near Lasea, and spent some time there. At this point Luke makes one of his allusions to the holy days the Church observed, noting that it was past the Day of Atonement (September/October), and thus sailing was becoming treacherous (verse 9). Paul's suggestion that they stay put for the winter was ignored, the Roman officer paying more attention to the pilot and the ship's owner, who wanted to head for Phoenix, a safer harbor in western Crete.

After a short time at sea, they were caught up in a fierce northeaster that drove them away from Crete. Passing a small island named Clauda, they had just enough respite to get the ship's small boat aboard before being driven toward the dangerous sandbars off Libya. Escaping this danger, the next day they began to jettison cargo and, on the third day, the ship's tackle. After many more storm-filled days, when it was hard to distinguish day from night, the crew and most passengers were at the point of giving up all hope. It was then that Paul stood up in their midst, reminding them that they should have listened when he warned of the dangers of sailing after a certain date. But now, he said, they need not fear; they would lose the ship but not their lives. He told them that during the previous night he had experienced a reassuring angelic vision. The message was that he would yet stand before Caesar, and that those traveling with him would be kept safe. All that was necessary was to find an island where they could run aground (verses 13–26).

On the 14th night the sailors sensed that land was near. Checking the depth, they found that the water was getting more and more shallow, and now they feared running into rocks during the night. Some of the crew tried to escape in the ship's small lifeboat. But Paul warned that only those who stayed on board would be saved. The soldiers then cut the boat adrift to prevent further escape attempts. In the morning, just before dawn, Paul advised them all to take food to regain strength for what lay ahead. He took some bread himself, gave thanks before them all, and ate it. The 276 people on board were encouraged, and after eating their fill, they threw all remaining grain overboard to lighten the vessel. The sailors pointed the ship toward a beach as daylight came and sailed straight ahead. Unfortunately they ran aground on a reef, where the sea was too strong. Soon the stern began to break apart in the pounding surf (verses 27–41).

The panicked soldiers wanted to kill the prisoners to prevent their escape. But the centurion wanted to keep Paul alive and so diverted the soldiers from their plan.

Directing those who could swim to jump overboard and head for the beach, he told the rest to take planks and pieces of the ship and float ashore.

And so they all arrived safely on the island of Malta.

Continuing Journey

For Paul it was at least his fourth experience of being shipwrecked. In his second letter to the Corinthian church, written well before this journey to Rome, he said, "Three times I was shipwrecked; a night and a day I was adrift at sea" (2 Corinthians 11:25). But on this occasion the local people came quickly to the rescue in the cold and rain, making fires to warm them.

Gathering some sticks and putting them on a fire, Paul was bitten on the hand by a poisonous snake, which he shook off into the flames. The superstitious locals thought he must be a murderer to be attacked this way and would therefore soon die. When after some time he didn't fall down, and in fact suffered no ill effects at all, they decided he must be a god (Acts 28:3–6).

The chief man on the island, Publius, invited Paul and his companions to his home and looked after them for three days. His father, who was very ill with fever and dysentery, recovered after Paul prayed and laid hands on him. As a result, many other sick people sought out the apostle.

When after three months of winter it was time to depart, the grateful locals gave Paul and his shipmates the things they needed to continue their journey (verses 7–10).

Finding a ship bound for Italy, they made a three-day stop at Syracuse, in Sicily, before proceeding past Rhegium and on to Puteoli on the Italian mainland. There they found fellow believers, and the centurion allowed them to stay for a week. As they approached Rome, Church members who had heard they were coming went to meet them. Some came out of Rome about 43 miles, or 70 kilometers, on the Appian Way to the Market of Appius, while others waited closer to the city at the Three Inns. Paul was much encouraged by this welcome.

Paul the Prisoner

Once in Rome, the apostle took up temporary lodgings (verse 23), perhaps at a friend's house. Soldiers, to whom he was attached by a chain (see verses 16 and 20), guarded him in shifts. Before long, however, he was able to live in his own rented accommodation for an extended period (verse 30). But even then, being chained to another man did not prevent him speaking out plainly. The fact that his freedom of speech was not limited tells us that this imprisonment was different than the one he alludes to in a late letter to his helper Timothy. At that time he was apparently also in Rome, but truly in jail.

On this occasion, after three days, Paul invited the local Jewish leaders to visit him. Their meeting gave him the opportunity to explain the circumstances surrounding his arrest, to proclaim his innocence, and to let his Jewish brothers know about the Messiah.

The emperor at the time of Paul's two-year imprisonment was the infamous Nero. It is likely that after receiving papers from Porcius Festus, he waited until he had heard from Paul's Jewish accusers in Jerusalem before meeting him. He perhaps also knew of Paul from his advisor Seneca, whose brother Gallio had heard and dismissed a complaint against the apostle lodged by other Jewish leaders in Corinth a few years earlier (Acts 18:12–16). But apparently the Jews in Rome knew nothing of the reason for Paul's recent arrival. They said, "We have received no letters from Judea about you, and none of the brothers coming here has reported or spoken any evil about you" (Acts 28:21). They were therefore open to hearing more about "this sect" that Paul represented, and which, they said, people were speaking against everywhere.

At a second meeting many people came to hear him, and he spoke from morning till night. He explained about the kingdom of God and the coming of the Messiah, using Hebrew Scripture ("the Law and the Prophets") to support his belief. Some were willing to hear, while others dismissed his teaching. Paul realized that a prophecy was being fulfilled at that moment and referred his listeners to the words found in Isaiah 6:9–10: "And he said, 'Go, and say to this people: "Keep on hearing, but do not understand; keep on seeing, but do not perceive." Make the heart of this people dull, and their ears heavy, and blind their eyes; lest they see with their eyes, and hear with their ears, and understand with their hearts, and turn and be healed.'"

Paul felt compelled to state that he would now go to the gentile peoples with the message, since his fellow Jews did not accept his teaching.

Thus, while he awaited his audience with Nero, Paul was able to receive all who came, "proclaiming the kingdom of God and teaching about the Lord Jesus Christ with all boldness and without hindrance" (Acts 28:31). This is an interesting division of responsibilities and provides food for thought. Paul had a twofold role: he was entrusted with both a public and a private work. His public work was that of preaching about, or announcing or proclaiming (Greek, *kerusso*), the coming of the kingdom of God on the earth. It was the same work that Jesus had done in His public role (see Mark 1:14). By contrast, the Greek word for teaching or instructing is *didasko*. This was the second aspect of both Jesus' and Paul's role. They taught a way of life to those who believed the announcement about the kingdom of God to prepare them for its establishment on the earth.

At this point Luke discontinues the account of the early Church that he has prepared for Theophilus, apparently because it is now current. Did Luke die before he could write a third volume? We simply do not know. But we can discover more about the apostle Paul in Rome, and by implication his release, from the letters he wrote during this two-year period.

Letters from Paul the Prisoner

Paul wrote several instructional letters that give an insight into both his pastoral care of the churches and his attention to a matter at the individual level.

He wrote to a wealthy Church member and friend named Philemon (Philemon 1), and also to congregations in three cities: Colossae, Ephesus and Philippi (see Colossians 4:3, 18; Ephesians 3:1; 4:1; 6:18–20; and Philippians 1:7, 12–17).

What can we learn from this correspondence?

Paul introduced himself to Philemon as "a prisoner for Christ Jesus" and well on in years (Philemon 1, 8–9) before asking for his indulgence in resolving a problem with one of his runaway slaves. The wrinkle in the situation was that the slave, Onesimus, had become a convert through Paul's prison ministry (verse 10) and was now returning with Paul's letter in hand (verse 12). Though the apostle could have used his authority to persuade Philemon to forgive his slave-become-brother and take him back, he rather entreated his friend, offering to cover any out-of-pocket costs or debts incurred by Onesimus (verses 18–19). Since the slave is mentioned as known to the church in Colossae—"who is one of you" (Colossians 4:9)—it is likely that Philemon also lived there.

Companions in Rome

As he signed off, Paul recorded for Philemon the names of several helpers, indicating that this imprisonment was not solitary. They include Epaphras, Mark, Aristarchus, Demas and Luke (verses 23–24). In his introduction, Paul had also mentioned Timothy, his spiritual son in the faith (see also Philippians 2:19, 22).

Epaphras was a tireless minister in the Colossian area, which also included congregations at nearby Laodicea and Hierapolis (Colossians 4:12–13). He had arrived in Rome bringing news of the state of the congregation at Colossae (Colossians 1:3–8). This caused Paul to compose a letter to them, which was carried back not by Epaphras, who stayed with Paul in Rome as his "fellow prisoner" (Philemon 23), but by Tychicus, "a beloved brother and faithful minister and fellow servant in the Lord," and the slave Onesimus (Colossians 4:7–9). Tychicus had traveled with Paul from

Greece to Jerusalem and was possibly an Ephesian (Acts 20:4). Perhaps this is the reason that Paul also entrusted him (Ephesians 6:21–22) with what is known to us as his letter to the Ephesians, though originally it may have been a circular letter destined for the churches that were centered around the capital city (early manuscripts do not contain the words "in Ephesus" [Ephesians 1:1], and its content is more general).

Mark was likely John Mark, who, as we know, had separated from Paul and Barnabas about 12 years earlier. His being with Paul now was an encouraging development in itself, and Paul later wrote to Timothy that "Mark . . . is very useful to me for ministry" (2 Timothy 4:11). An early tradition holds that Mark wrote the Gospel by his name for the Romans. Being present in Rome with Paul gives some support for that belief.

Aristarchus was a Thessalonian convert who had accompanied Paul on various other journeys (see Acts 19:29; 20:4), as well as on the voyage to Rome. Paul mentioned him also as "my fellow prisoner" in Rome (Colossians 4:10).

Demas, later described as "in love with this present world," eventually deserted Paul (2 Timothy 4:10), whereas Luke, "the beloved physician" (Colossians 4:14) and author of both the Gospel by his name and the book of Acts, remained faithful to the end. He traveled with Paul to Rome on this occasion and also for his second and final imprisonment there.

In Colossians, Paul commends another helper, the Jewish convert Jesus (Justus), who was also close to him in his imprisonment.

Sometime during Paul's stay in Rome, Epaphroditus from Philippi visited him. This resulted in the letter known as Philippians. Paul commended his visitor for his extraordinary assistance, "for he nearly died for the work of Christ, risking his life to complete what was lacking in your service to me" (Philippians 2:30). Once recovered, Epaphroditus returned to his home congregation with Paul's letter (verse 25).

Thus we know that Paul was not alone in Rome in such difficult circumstances but was surrounded by several faithful and true brothers, not to mention the Church members who were residents of the capital (see Romans 16), and for whom he wrote the extended doctrinal book of Romans.

Success Under Duress

Despite the limitations on his freedom, Paul was intent on finding ways to continue the work of proclaiming the good news about God's coming kingdom and the role Jesus had played in making reconciliation with the Father possible. He asked the members in Colossae and Ephesus to "pray also for us, that God may open to us a door for the word, to [boldly] declare the mystery of Christ, on account of which I am in prison" (Colossians 4:3; see also Ephesians 6:19). He also mentioned to the Philippians that "it has become known throughout the whole imperial guard and to all the rest that my imprisonment is for Christ" (Philippians 1:13). As we have noted, Paul was likely chained to various guards day and night (see Ephesians 6:20 and Acts 28:20, which mention a chain, or manacles); thus his every word would have been overheard.

And it was not only among the imperial guard that Paul's message became known. At the close of his letter to the congregation at Philippi, he wrote, "All the saints greet you, especially those of Caesar's household" (Philippians

4:22). Were these newly converted people Nero's servants or relatives? Unfortunately, there is no way of knowing.

Paul fully expected that he would be released from this imprisonment. Hence his comment to Philemon, "Prepare a guest room for me" (Philemon 22), and to the Philippians, "I trust in the Lord that shortly I myself will come also" (Philippians 2:24).

Overlapping Messages

In the three congregational letters, Paul covered several overlapping themes. In Ephesians and Colossians, there is the reminder that it is only by special revelation from God that the Church understands what it does of His great purpose in creating humanity and sending Jesus Christ. Paul referred to this as a mystery (Greek, *musterion*). The word signifies a secret, a hidden truth that is God's alone to reveal if and when He chooses and to whomever He chooses. Paul emphasized that God had called certain individuals from the gentile world, as well as the Jewish world, to participate in a relationship with Him through Jesus Christ. This development had been hidden until the first century, when God chose to reveal it. It was, as Paul said, "the mystery hidden for ages and generations but now revealed to his saints" (Colossians 1:26), "which was not made known to the sons of men . . . as it has now been revealed to his holy apostles and prophets by the Spirit" (Ephesians 3:5). It was Paul's specific responsibility to let this be known to those whom God had called in the gentile world, and as a result he was now a prisoner (Ephesians 3:1).

All three letters make reference to the need for boldness in proclaiming the good news of the kingdom of God and

Jesus Christ. As we have seen, Paul asked that the members in Colossae pray for him to be able to speak his message plainly and openly (Colossians 4:3). Similarly, he asked those to whom the Ephesian letter went for prayers that he would speak out boldly (Ephesians 6:19–20). He commended the members in Rome for doing just that themselves as a result of his imprisonment (Philippians 1:14) and expressed his hope that he, too, would act with boldness in answer to their prayers for him (verses 19–20).

Further, Paul was joyful in his suffering, because he knew that it had a great purpose not only for himself but also for the membership (Colossians 1:24; Ephesians 3:13). He did not want them to be discouraged by his situation, because he believed that it would all turn out for the good (Philippians 1:19).

Ephesians, Colossians and Philemon contain general instruction for the God-fearing family and for masters and slaves (Ephesians 5:22–6:9; Colossians 3:18–4:1; Philemon 10–18). Husbands and wives and children are encouraged to treat each other with mutual respect (Paul demonstrates in his letters to the Ephesians and the Colossians that he was far from the woman-hater that many have painted him to be). Converted masters are to treat slaves with fairness, and converted slaves are to work honorably.

Specific Messages

While there are overlaps in the letters, when it comes to the specific reasons for each letter, there are also differences. As we have seen already, Paul responded to the circumstances that were presented to him in respect of the congregations in Colossae and Philippi.

Judging by Paul's letter to the Colossians, Epaphras had come with some serious concerns about their spiritual well-being. It seems that the brethren were being swayed by Greek philosophical ideas (Colossians 2:8). One of the central precepts concerned spirits who were said to rule the world and mediate between humans and God. According to this philosophy, such beings deserved worship, which included ascetic practices (Colossians 2:18). Paul sought to free the Colossians from this error by reminding them that followers of Jesus had no need for such human beliefs and practices. He wrote, "If with Christ you died to the elemental spirits of the world, why, as if you were still alive in the world, do you submit to regulations—'Do not handle, Do not taste, Do not touch' (referring to things that perish as they are used)—according to human precepts and teachings?" (Colossians 2:20–22). This, he insisted, is "self-made religion" (verse 23) that might look appealing but is in fact an "empty deceit" (verse 8).

Philippians was written in response to Epaphroditus visiting Paul in prison and bringing news of the congregation. It is a letter filled with gratitude on Paul's part for the brethren's spiritual development. He took the opportunity to teach them about the mind and attitude of Christ, which they should emulate. It is a humble mind that does nothing from motives of rivalry or conceit and seeks the good of others, willing to lay down life itself for them (Philippians 2:1–8). As followers of Jesus Christ, the Philippians were to live honorably on earth as citizens of the kingdom of heaven yet to come (Philippians 1:27).

As already mentioned, the letter we know as Ephesians was possibly meant for circulation in the region around the city, including places such as Laodicea, Hierapolis and Colossae, where Paul mentioned that Church congregations existed and letters were exchanged (Colossians 4:13, 16). It is a more general letter than either Colossians or Philippians and deals with expansive themes in God's plan. It explains the centrality of Jesus Christ's life, death and resurrection to that plan (chapter 1) and includes His calling some to conversion in this life, ahead of others (chapters 2–3). It teaches the vital importance of unity among the believers and how they are educated and protected in God's way (chapters 4–6).

Thus we see that Paul's two-year house arrest in Rome was not spent idly, nor did the congregations in his care suffer from lack of attention from the aged apostle.

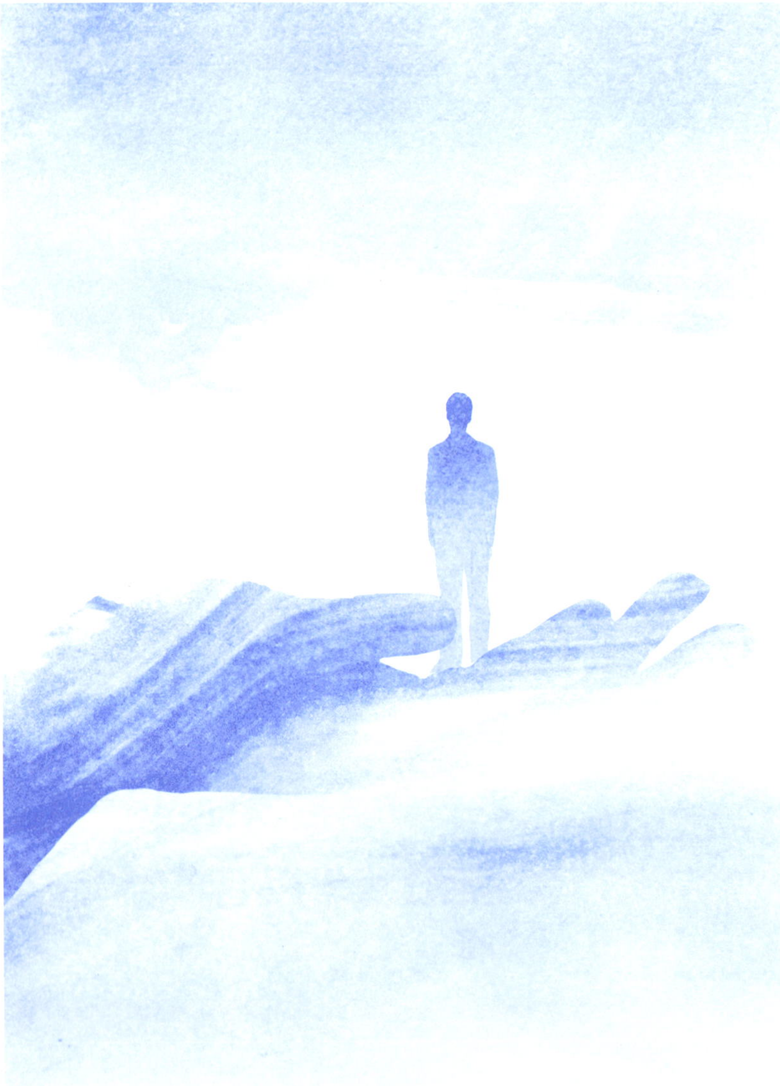

Journeys' End

The character traits of those suitable for ministerial work make for a list of very demanding attributes. . . . They must be exemplary individuals, chosen after careful consideration.

From a letter to his helper Timothy we know that Paul was held captive a second and final time. What happened between his first and second periods in prison forms a very important though little-known part of Paul's life. During this time he demonstrated his ongoing care for the churches, traveling to several cities and writing the personal letters that became the New Testament books of 1 Timothy and Titus.

People and Places

In his second letter to Timothy, written from prison, the apostle mentions his final detention and impending death. He also mentions a visitor, Onesiphorus, who according to Paul had been with him in Rome at his first imprisonment and had helped him later in Ephesus (2 Timothy 1:16–18). Thus we know that Paul went to Ephesus after his first stay in the capital. This is confirmed in the first letter to Timothy, where the apostle writes, "I urged you when I was going to Macedonia, remain at Ephesus so that you may charge certain persons not to teach any different doctrine" (1 Timothy 1:3). We know that the Church experienced increasing internal difficulties with the spread of heretical teachings, and this becomes clear throughout Paul's letters.

During the interval of freedom between Roman imprisonments, Paul was also in several places with other colleagues. He was in Crete with Titus (Titus 1:5), in Troas with Carpus (2 Timothy 4:13), in Corinth with Erastus, and in Miletus with Trophimus (2 Timothy 4:20). Further, he tells Titus that he will spend a winter in Nicopolis on the Adriatic Sea, where his "true child in a common faith" should come (Titus 1:4; 3:12).

When Paul was in Rome during his first imprisonment, he indicated at different times that when set free he would go to Spain (Romans 15:24, 28), Philippi (Philippians 1:26; 2:24) and Colossae (Philemon 22), and if to Colossae, then he might possibly go to nearby Laodicea and Hierapolis (Colossians 2:1; 4:12-13). Whether he actually made these journeys is not known for sure, though his words indicate his genuine concern for all the churches and for the preaching of the good news far and wide (see also 2 Corinthians 11:28; 1 Corinthians 9:16).

Appointing Leaders

A common theme in 1 Timothy and Titus concerns the selection and ordination of Church leadership for the effective organization of local congregations. Paul gives instruction to his two colleagues who are facing similar problems though in very different places—Ephesus and Crete. They are to choose certain qualified men for the work of ministerial service, and similar men and women as deacons.

The character traits of those suitable for ministerial work make for a list of very demanding attributes (1 Timothy 3:1-7; Titus 1:5-9). Such persons are to be of good reputation, experienced in the faith, sober minded, hospitable, capable of teaching and sound in doctrinal understanding, faithful husbands, and responsible fathers in charge of their own homes. They cannot be drunkards, materialistic, aggressive or argumentative. In sum, they must be exemplary individuals, chosen after careful consideration (1 Timothy 5:22).

If complaints against elders should arise, Paul determined that the right course would be to establish the facts in the presence of two or three witnesses. He did this to avoid partiality toward either party—members or ministers. Ministers are to be respected for the work they do and rewarded accordingly, both financially and in terms of honor shown (1 Timothy 5:17–21).

With such leadership in place, the congregations would have the best possibility of stability in the midst of religious and philosophical confusion. And such a world it was. Ephesus was a hotbed of competing ideas. Crete was known for an unsavory approach to life. The Cretan poet Epimenides (ca. 600 B.C.E.) said all Cretans were "liars, evil brutes, lazy gluttons." Paul mentioned this to Titus (1:12) because it seems that the Cretan mentality had infected members of the long-established Jewish community and that it had perhaps rubbed off on some in the early Church.

Battling Heresies and Heretics

A second dominant theme in both letters concerns the need to be on guard against encroaching heresies. The longer the Church existed, the more it seems that it came under pressure from those with opposing doctrines. It's apparent that by the 60s C.E. the teachings of the early Church were being subverted throughout the Roman world and that Paul believed the way to counter the trend was through ministerial intervention and sound teaching.

Paul advises his younger helpers about dealing with such difficulties. He tells Timothy to warn those followers involved in doctrinal diversions "[not] to devote themselves to myths and endless genealogies, which promote speculations rather than the stewardship from God that is by faith" (1 Timothy 1:4). To Titus he says, "There are many who are insubordinate, empty talkers and deceivers, especially those of the circumcision party. They must be silenced, since they are upsetting whole families by teaching for shameful gain what they ought not to teach" (Titus 1:10–11; see also 3:9). This desire for gain is not a mark of a true teacher of Christ. As Paul writes to Timothy, "those who desire to be rich fall into temptation, into a snare, into many senseless and harmful desires that plunge people into ruin and destruction. For the love of money is a root of all kinds of evils. It is through this craving that some have wandered away from the faith and pierced themselves with many pangs" (1 Timothy 6:9–10).

Paul names two individuals who caused division with their heretical ideas—Hymenaeus and Alexander—who "concerning the faith have suffered shipwreck" (1 Timothy 1:19–20, NKJV). Paul mentions Hymenaeus again in his second letter to Timothy, where the problem is defined: the heretic was teaching "that the resurrection has already happened," with the result that he was "upsetting the faith of some" (2 Timothy 2:17–18). Under these circumstances Paul acted decisively to protect the Church. He says, "I have handed [Hymenaeus and Alexander] over to Satan that they may learn not to blaspheme" (1 Timothy 1:20). It was no doubt a form of excommunication for the purpose of reform. This accords with his advice to Titus in such situations: "As for a person who stirs up division, after warning him once and then twice, have nothing more to do with him, knowing that such a person is warped and sinful; he is self-condemned" (Titus 3:10–11).

The Godly Community

A third theme in these two pastoral letters is encouragement to teach all members of the congregations about their responsibilities in the Church community (1 Timothy 5:1–15; Titus 2:2–10). Whether older or younger, men or women, ordained or not, all need to play a harmonious role.

Paul reminds Timothy of part of his reason for writing to him: "so that . . . you may know how one ought to behave in the household of God, which is the church of the living God, a pillar and buttress of truth" (1 Timothy 3:14–15). He tells him to "set the believers an example in speech, in conduct, in love, in faith, in purity" (1 Timothy 4:12). That Timothy and Titus were both younger men is shown by Paul's addressing each as "my true child" (1 Timothy 1:2; Titus 1:4) and by his urging that no one be allowed to despise their youth and/or authority (1 Timothy 4:12; Titus 2:15).

To Titus Paul says, "Show yourself in all respects to be a model of good works, and in your teaching show integrity, dignity, and sound speech that cannot be condemned, so that an opponent may be put to shame, having nothing evil to say about us" (Titus 2:7–8).

It is clear from the extensive instructions given that Paul speaks from a great deal of personal experience in handling problems in human relationships. For example, he advises Timothy how to approach older and younger men and women as their teacher. He says, "Do not rebuke an older man but encourage him as you would a father, younger men as brothers, older women as mothers, younger women as sisters, in all purity" (1 Timothy 5:1–2).

Titus must teach older men to demonstrate serious-mindedness, dignity and self-control, having faith, love and steadfastness. Older women are to be taught likewise, with the additional cautions to avoid gossip and too much wine. They also have the opportunity to contribute to the community of believers by teaching younger women about marriage, motherhood and running a home. Self-control is also high on the agenda for younger women, as it is for younger men (Titus 2:1–6).

Paul's emphasis to Timothy as regards the women in the Church is similar in parts but different in others in that it also concentrates on the care of widows. He is careful to distinguish those who are really in need of Church help and those who are young enough to remarry, have children and take care of themselves. He is also concerned that all in the Church should carry out their obligations to widows within their individual families. Not to do so is a serious failing: "If anyone does not provide for his relatives, and especially for members of his household, he has denied the faith and is worse than an unbeliever" (1 Timothy 5:8).

Slaves or bondservants were a part of the Roman-dominated world, and Paul addresses the matter of how those slaves who were also followers of Jesus should behave. He says that they should "regard their own masters as worthy of all honor, so that the name of God and the teaching may not be reviled" (1 Timothy 6:1). To Titus he writes, "Slaves are to be submissive to their own masters in everything; they are to be well-pleasing, not argumentative, not pilfering, but showing all good faith, so that in everything they may adorn the doctrine of God our Savior" (Titus 2:9–10). Was this because Paul approved of slavery? No, for he writes elsewhere, "If you can gain your freedom, avail yourself of the opportunity." But showing that there is something far more important than station in life, he prefaces that comment: "Were you a slave when called? Do not be concerned about it" (1 Corinthians 7:21). In the case of those slaves whose masters are also believers, he says, "Those who have believing masters must not be disrespectful on the ground that they are brothers; rather they must serve all the better since those who benefit by their good service are believers and beloved" (1 Timothy 6:2).

All of this instruction paints the picture of a community that is being taught to be at peace with itself, knowing that it lives temporarily in a difficult world that will be eclipsed by the coming of Christ: "For the grace of God has appeared, bringing salvation for all people, training us to renounce ungodliness and worldly passions, and to live self-controlled, upright, and godly lives in the present age, waiting for our blessed hope, the appearing of the glory of our great God and Savior Jesus Christ, who gave himself for us to redeem us from all lawlessness and to purify for himself a people for his own possession who are zealous for good works" (Titus 2:11–14).

Final Words

Sometime during his travels, probably after his winter stay in Nicopolis, en route to or at Troas, Paul was taken prisoner and transported once more to Rome (2 Timothy 4:13). There he wrote the last letter that we have, known as 2 Timothy. The situation vis-à-vis the followers of Jesus had changed. Nero had now launched his persecution against the growing numbers of Christians (these were not likely the same as the followers of Jesus but more probably those who followed some of the corrupters of the faith that Paul warned Timothy and Titus about). As we now know, *Christian* was not a term that the followers of Jesus used of themselves. Yet the antagonism caused by these Christians in Rome spread, and

Paul was evidently caught in the net. He writes to Timothy that he is suffering imprisonment in Rome, "bound with chains as a criminal" for preaching the good news of Jesus Christ (2 Timothy 1:17; 2:8–9). Paul has had one hearing during which time no one came to his defense. He has been remanded and awaits his sentence (2 Timothy 4:16).

As noted earlier, he has been visited and encouraged by Onesiphorus. Now he turns to encouraging Timothy, his "beloved child." It is remarkable that under these difficult prison conditions Paul is able to write with such clear focus and conviction. He has been deserted by many of his helpers: "You are aware that all who are in Asia turned away from me, among whom are Phygelus and Hermogenes" (2 Timothy 1:15). Demas, who won praise in Paul's first letter to Timothy, has also left him and gone to Thessalonica "in love with this present world." Two other helpers who are without condemnation have traveled to distant places: "Crescens has gone to Galatia, Titus to Dalmatia" (2 Timothy 4:10). In his lonely state, with only Luke remaining, Paul is anxious to see Timothy and Mark in Rome soon. He asks for his cloak left behind in Troas—protection, no doubt, against the dank cold of prison life—and for his books and parchments. This may be a reference to his copies of Hebrew and Greek texts and his collected letters.

Facing almost certain death, Paul reminds Timothy again of his continuing ministerial responsibility to protect the flock in the face of spreading heresies. He knows that false teachers will continue to arise and that people will warm to such imposters. He warns his colleague of this reality, as he did the Ephesian elders in earlier days. But with his approaching death, the apostle says that he is prepared for the inevitable: "For I am already being poured out as a drink offering, and the time of my departure has come" (2 Timothy 4:6).

Paul's remarkable life in God's service, from his unique calling on the Damascus Road, to the revelations in Arabia; the 14 silent years until his rediscovery by Barnabas; the appearances before rulers, a king and an emperor; the journeys on foot of ten thousand miles; the beatings; the shipwrecks; the persecutions—all of this he summarizes in the statement: "I have fought the good fight, I have finished the race, I have kept the faith. Henceforth there is laid up for me the crown of righteousness, which the Lord, the righteous judge, will award to me on that Day, and not only to me but also to all who have loved his appearing" (2 Timothy 4:7-8).

Tradition holds that Paul was beheaded in Rome around 67-68 C.E. on Nero's orders but while the emperor was absent from the capital. It's further said that a Roman matron named Lucina sought out his body for burial in her vineyard. A church was built on the site in the time of the emperor Constantine and included a tomb with an inscription on marble that read *Paulo Apostolo Mart[yri]*, "the martyr, the Apostle Paul." Today it lies underneath the church of *San Paolo Fuori le Mura* (St. Paul Outside the Walls).

There is no separate confirmation of any of the traditions surrounding the apostle's death and burial. What is known is found in Luke's extensive account of Paul's life, aided by the content of the apostle's own letters.

… Chapter Seven

James, Brother of Jesus

It is like looking at our image in the mirror, seeing what is wrong, and doing nothing to remedy what we find.

Our main sources thus far have been the Acts of the Apostles, written by Paul's travel companion Luke, and Paul's own letters. Of the original 12 apostles, Judas Iscariot had already committed suicide (Matthew 27:1–5) and is not even mentioned by name in Acts; the remaining 11 are named only once (Acts 1:13). Nevertheless, with Matthias replacing Judas (verse 26), Luke refers to them as a renewed group of 12 (Acts 6:2; see also 6:6; 4:33; 5:18, 29; 15:2; 16:4). Among them in the early days of the Church were also several women (including Jesus' mother, Mary) and His brothers (Acts 1:14).

But Acts is not the only source of information about some of the individuals closest to Jesus. Like Paul, they are also known through their own writings. Letters written by Simon Peter, John, James and Jude form part of the New Testament. In this chapter we explore the biography and written work of James.

Which James?

We noted previously that in the early days of the Church, about 44 C.E., King Herod Agrippa killed the apostle James, the son of Zebedee and one of the original twelve (see Acts 12:1–2). Thus it must be another James to whom Luke refers in verse 17 of the same chapter, where he records that Peter sent news of his release from prison to someone named James. Though as many as seven different people by the same name have been identified in the New Testament, it is James the brother of Jesus (Galatians 1:19) who is the most likely in this case. As we have just seen, Jesus' brothers were present with the apostles in Jerusalem as the Church began after Jesus' departure (Acts 1:14). This same James appears later in Acts as the leader of the church at Jerusalem, so it's reasonable to suggest that he is the author of the New Testament book by that name.

As leader in Jerusalem, James spoke with authority to end an internal Church controversy over the circumcision of gentile believers (Acts 15:13–19; see also 21:18). And according to the first-century Jewish historian Josephus, the Jewish religious hierarchy put to death by stoning "the brother of Jesus, who was called Christ, whose name was James" (*Antiquities of the Jews* 20.200). This would have been around 62 C.E.

But was this James also an apostle? While he is never named directly as such in the New Testament, the argument has been made that his family relationship to Jesus accorded him a unique role. Paul, who himself became an apostle but was not of the twelve, seems to indicate James's apostolic function when writing about one of his visits to Jerusalem. He says, "I saw none of the other apostles except James the Lord's brother" (Galatians 1:19). But scholars have suggested that this is not an unequivocal statement. An alternate translation says, "Other than the apostles I saw no one except James, the Lord's brother."

James the Unbeliever

What more can we know of James and his earlier life from the Gospel accounts? Mark and Matthew indicate that he was one of several children born to Mary and Joseph after Jesus' birth. Mark records an incident in Jesus' ministry where his fellow townsmen derided Him as merely a local: "'Is not this the carpenter, the son of Mary and brother of James and Joses and Judas and Simon? And are not his sisters here with us?' And they took offense at him" (Mark 6:3; see also Matthew 13:55–56).

There was a time when James and his brothers were opposed to Jesus' ministry and teaching. John tells us that "not even his brothers believed in him" (John 7:5).

By the opening of the book of Acts, however, James had become one of the disciples. But even though he was Jesus' brother, he did not take up the vacancy caused by Judas's death, because the remaining 11 were to choose as a witness to Jesus' resurrection "one of the men who ha[d] accompanied [them] during all the time that the Lord Jesus went in and out among [them]" (Acts 1:21). James soon became the leader of the Jerusalem church, as demonstrated by the fact that Paul met with him and the apostle Peter, also called Cephas, when he first went to Jerusalem after his conversion (Galatians 1:18–19). He met James on another occasion when he brought famine relief to Jerusalem from the churches outside Judea (Acts 21:18).

The fact that James was leader in Jerusalem is attested by such extrabiblical sources as the second-century historian Hegesippus. He wrote that following James's death, the Church chose another of Jesus' blood relatives, His cousin Simon or Simeon, to be leader—thus implying that up to that time James had held the post. According to Eusebius, another reference is found in the (now lost) writings of Clement of Alexandria (ca. 153–217 C.E.), who says that Peter and John chose James for his office (*Books of the Hypotyposes* 6). And writing in 492, Jerome says that James "ruled the church of Jerusalem thirty years, that is until the seventh year of Nero" (*Lives of Illustrious Men*, chapter 2).

It was in this capacity that James most likely wrote the letter by his name.

James's Tour de Force

The short book of James is a moral, doctrinal and literary masterpiece. While some have thought its content at odds with the writings of Paul, its emphasis on living according to "the perfect law," "the law of liberty" and "the royal law" (James 1:25; 2:8) places it firmly within the same Judaic tradition. Close examination of its central concepts reveals the complementary nature of each man's thinking.

James opens by emphasizing his submission to "God and . . . the Lord Jesus Christ," addressing his audience across a wide geographic area: "To the twelve tribes in the Dispersion: Greetings" (James 1:1). Coming from a Jewish background, James was aware of the history of ancient Israel and its origins with the 12 sons of Jacob. That many of their descendants, not just those from the tribe of Judah, had been dispersed through captivity, persecution and migration explains his reference. James was writing to Church members descended from these tribes in what was considered the area of the Diaspora—today's Mediterranean and Middle Eastern regions (see also Acts 2:9-11; 1 Peter 1:1; John 7:35).

The followers of Jesus in any age have one experience in common—they face trials of faith for a great purpose, and James addresses this at the outset of his letter: "The testing of your faith produces steadfastness" (James 1:3), which in turn brings spiritual completion in the form of eternal life ("the crown of life," verse 12). Thus he contextualizes trying circumstances in the light of spiritual development. And if trials cause us to recognize our need for wisdom in dealing with them, then we should ask God for such help in confidence. Double-mindedness achieves nothing; quiet trust in God's guidance and help is the key (verses 5–8). Wealth affords little protection against these kinds of problems. The rich will eventually fade like the grass of the field (verses 9–11).

James further cautions against falling into the trap of blaming God for the difficulties we bring on ourselves by succumbing to sin (verses 13–15). God gives good gifts to His children, not the evil consequences of our own wrong actions. Thankfully, He is unlike fallible and variable humanity: He is "the Father of lights with whom there is no variation or shadow due to change." We can rely on Him implicitly if we so choose. He is the one who has willed that His people be given truth in *this* life, before others receive it, so that they will become "a kind of firstfruits of his creatures" (verses 17–18).

James's emphasis on the practice of right living is found early in the letter. At the close of the first chapter he sets the tone for what will follow. He draws the contrast between natural human ways of behaving—we are slow to hear, quick to speak and quickly angry—and God's ways. Human anger cannot produce godly righteousness. It is the Word of God that instructs us in right ways. But knowing is not enough, he writes; we must act on what we know to be right. Otherwise it is like looking at our image in the mirror, seeing what is wrong, and doing nothing to remedy what we find (verses 23–24). Thus, defining meaningful religion, James expresses its core in terms of both self-control and positive, outgoing action. He says, "If anyone thinks he is religious and does not bridle his tongue but deceives his heart, this person's religion is worthless. Religion that is pure and undefiled before God, the Father, is this: to visit orphans and widows in their affliction, and to keep oneself unstained from the world" (verses 26–27). The theme of acting on belief will recur throughout the letter.

Practical Outcomes

The law of God covers all aspects of human behavior in principle, and James gives several examples of how belief should result in changed, law-abiding behavior. First, he writes that favoring one person over another according to his or her wealth and status has no place in the godly value system (James 2:1–9). After all, he says, it is too often the wealthy who exploit and disadvantage the poor. They may even disparage the name of Jesus.

James's example involves two men coming into the meeting of Jesus' followers as visitors. One is well dressed and wealthy, the other shabbily dressed and poor. James says that respecting the first over the other because of wealth and social standing would be wrong. It would be dishonoring and humiliating the poor. Showing partiality is breaking one part of the law by not loving neighbor as self—one of the two great overall principles of the Ten Commandments (see Matthew 22:35–40). And breaking law is sin. It is a biblical concept that keeping all but one law still renders us accountable. For example, James says, by refusing to commit adultery, but on the other hand committing murder, it is as if we are guilty of breaking the whole law (James 2:10–11). The idea here is that the law cannot be divided into important and less important commands. We must adhere to all of it, realizing that God will judge us according to its principles, which, if kept in the spirit, free us from the penalty of sin: eternal death (verse 12). James concludes by stating that those who show mercy, love and justice (to the poor, in this example) will receive mercy in the judgment.

He gives a second example of the requirement for faith to be demonstrated in action, pointing out the needs of those members of the believing community who are going hungry. It is a form of hypocrisy to hear their pleas, express hope for their eventual nourishment, and yet do nothing practical to help. Faith must be proven by works. Without them faith is dead (verses 14–17). Citing the case of Abraham, James shows that the patriarch's faith was accompanied by works, and as a result he became known as the friend of God (verse 23). Faith alone is insufficient.

In a third example of belief demonstrated by action, James turns in chapter three to an extended discussion of the need to bridle or control the tongue, a subject he has touched on earlier (James 1:19, 26). He begins by mentioning that teaching is a hazardous occupation, because those who do it are responsible for what they say, and it is easy to say things imperfectly (James 3:1–2). For this reason alone people should not be too ambitious to become teachers. Further, we will all be judged in part by what we say.

The difficulty of controlling the tongue is contrasted with how easily we guide much larger objects. We lead a horse by putting a bit into its mouth and steer a ship with a rudder. Small things can control big objects. But the tongue, which is also small in comparison to the body, is itself very difficult to control. Its effect can be like a small spark in a dry forest. The tongue is likened to a fire that can set nature ablaze. Instead of guiding the body, the tongue often causes it great trouble, ruining the whole person. Humans have tamed or controlled all other creatures, but the tongue is very hard to tame; like a snake, "it is a restless evil, full of deadly poison" (verse 8).

The paradox, says James, is that we bless God with the tongue but at the same time use it to curse our fellow humans who are made in His image. This is plainly wrong. A spring doesn't produce both fresh and salt water, nor a fig tree olives, nor a grapevine figs, nor a salt pond fresh water (verses 11–12).

How do humans then manage to bridle the tongue? It requires a special kind of wisdom that has to be acted out in everyday life (verse 13). James shows that it's only by connection with God that we can attain this wisdom and thus overcome the almost overwhelming inclination to misuse the tongue. Jealousy and selfish ambition find expression through the tongue, but the wisdom that comes "from above" produces an attitude that is "pure, then peaceable, gentle, open to reason, full of mercy and good fruits, impartial and sincere" (verse 17). This prevents "earthly, unspiritual [and] demonic" behavior (verse 15). Peacemaking brings with it an abundance of right action (verse 18).

Yet James's audience is experiencing quarrels and strife. He asks where such problems originate (James 4:1). His answer is that they come from within the human heart that is frustrated by not getting what it wants—though too often it wants what it ought not to have. To achieve its ends it will murder fellowman or go to war. This approach has no possibility of bringing satisfaction. Even when they do ask God for things, they do not receive them because they are asking from wrong motivations or for wrong things. If they follow the world's ways to gain their desires, they can only be enemies of God, the equivalent of adulterers in their commitment toward Him (verse 4). James exhorts them to become humble, submit to God, resist the devil—in sum, to change their ways (verses 7–10). One of the problems they have is speaking evil of and judging each other. They are rather to judge themselves and become "doers of the law" (verses 11–12).

James next issues a warning against pursuing materialistic goals as if nothing can go wrong. It is folly to act as if we know what tomorrow will bring. Life itself is ephemeral. We are dependent on God's mercy and His will and should recognize Him in all our planning (verses 13–15). Knowing the right way and failing to practice it is sin, he says. This is an evil that will not go unpunished.

Similarly, wealthy people are cautioned to get their priorities right. Gold and silver will be worthless one day, because the last days of human civilization are approaching. Then all of the material goods will be of no benefit. Too often they have been gained at the expense of hired workers, but fraud and self-indulgence will have their end.

In such a world the followers of James's elder Brother are to demonstrate patience until His return. Like the farmer who must wait for his crops to receive seasonal rains and then mature, so they must hold fast to their belief and practice until "the coming of the Lord" (James 5:7–8). There is no time for the petty grumbling and complaining against each other that humans so easily take up. If they need a model of patience in suffering, they should reflect on the history of the prophets. For examples of perseverance in difficult circumstances, James writes, they should consider

Job, knowing that God is compassionate and merciful (verses 9–11). Their commitment should be simple and sincere, exemplified by honest communication: "Let your 'yes' be yes and your 'no' be no, so that you may not fall under condemnation" (verse 12).

Closing Thoughts

James's letter closes with the same emphasis on practical expressions of faith: If there are those among the believers who are suffering, they should pray to God about it. If there are those who are happy, they should express praise to God. Those who are ill should call for the elders of the Church and ask for prayer and anointing so that God may heal them. If sin has caused their illness, they will be forgiven; prayer and the confession of sin are essential to healing. The prayers of the righteous for others are very effective. James cites the example of Elijah (1 Kings 17, 18), who prayed that it would not rain. His prayers were so effective that God held back the rain for three and a half years. When the time had passed, he prayed that the rains would come, and they did.

In conclusion, James explains that one of the most valuable things we can do for fellow followers of the way of God is to bring them back from error. It is a practice that produces great reward. "Let him know that whoever brings back a sinner from his wandering will save his soul from death and will cover a multitude of sins" (verse 20). This conclusion confirms James's concern for the community of believers he had become a part of and led following the death and resurrection of Jesus. It is an early and powerful letter from one whose life was lived in the shadow of Jesus of Nazareth.

Chapter Eight

Feed My Sheep!
"And when the chief Shepherd appears, you will receive the unfading crown of glory."

In this survey of Jesus' apostles, we have come once more to the towering figure of Peter. The early part of his biography is found in the four Gospels. His middle years are accounted for in the book of Acts. But there are yet more aspects of his life and teaching to be gleaned from other New Testament books. Before doing that, let's recap the essentials.

Jesus Himself gave Simon, a Galilean fisherman, the name by which he's best known. He "looked at him and said, 'So you are Simon the son of John? You shall be called Cephas' (which means Peter)" (John 1:42). These names, Aramaic and Greek respectively, both mean "rock." Peter is also referred to as Simon Bar-Jonah (Matthew 16:17) and Simon or Simeon Peter (John 1:40; 2 Peter 1:1).

If Mark's Gospel was indeed the earliest written, as many scholars think, then we first meet Peter there. Alternatively, the several references to "Cephas" in Paul's letter to the Galatians may be the earliest written mention of him, as some scholars believe that Paul wrote to the church in Galatia before any of the Gospels or other epistles were set down. And Paul is consistent in his use (see 1 Corinthians) with only a couple of exceptions in Galatians.

Paul says that three years after his own conversion, he "went up to Jerusalem to visit Cephas and remained with him fifteen days" (Galatians 1:18; see also Acts 9:26–30). At this point, early in Church history, Cephas/Peter is specified as the main contact. This is understandable from several perspectives. As Paul later noted, Cephas was the first apostolic witness of Christ's resurrection. He wrote, "I delivered to you as of first importance what I also received: that Christ died for our sins in accordance with the Scriptures, that he was buried, that he was raised on the third day in accordance with the Scriptures, and that he appeared to Cephas, then to the twelve" (1 Corinthians 15:3–5).

This is indicated and confirmed in the Gospel accounts. The women who visited the tomb only to find it empty were told: "Do not be alarmed. You seek Jesus of Nazareth, who was crucified. He has risen; he is not here. See the place where they laid him. But go, tell his disciples and Peter that he is going before you to Galilee" (Mark 16:6–7). Peter is again singled out.

The apostle John's account is similar; it, too, emphasizes Peter's role in discovering Jesus' resurrection (John 20:1–8).

The Gospel writer Luke makes reference to Peter in the account of two men who met the resurrected Jesus on the road from Jerusalem to nearby Emmaus. Only after they sat down to eat together with Jesus and He disappeared from view did they realize who the stranger among them was. Shocked, "they rose that same hour and returned to Jerusalem. And they found the eleven and those who were with them gathered together, saying, 'The Lord has risen indeed, and has appeared to Simon!'" (Luke 24:33–34).

The Middle Years

When Paul went back to Jerusalem after 14 years, he again met Peter. But this time it was to resolve a growing contention in the early Church—the idea that to become followers of Jesus, non-Jews must be circumcised. Paul had taught that physical circumcision was not necessary for adult gentile believers. To be sure that his teaching was in accord with that of the other apostles in Jerusalem, he went to see them privately. The result, he says, was that "when they saw that I had been entrusted with the gospel to the uncircumcised, just as Peter had been entrusted with the gospel to the circumcised . . . James and Cephas and John . . . gave the right hand of fellowship to Barnabas and me, that we should go to the Gentiles and they to the circumcised" (Galatians 2:7–9).

It is noticeable that Cephas is no longer the only apostle mentioned by name. Here he is listed as one of three, with James first in order. It may well be that by this time James, the brother of Jesus, had come to the fore as the leader of the Jerusalem church while the apostles traveled.

In his letter to the Galatians, Paul is trying to set the congregations straight on a few points of doctrine. The reference he makes to recent Church history is to support his case that what he has taught them is in fact in line with official teaching. He mentions Cephas specifically, because Paul's opponents may have been using his poor example to support their case for circumcision. He continues, "When Cephas came to Antioch, I opposed him to his face, because he stood condemned. For before certain men came from James, he was eating with the Gentiles; but when they came he drew back and separated himself, fearing the circumcision party" (Galatians 2:11–12).

So at this point, Peter displayed a partiality toward the gentile converts that did not match his belief and experience. He was being hypocritical and leading others, such as Barnabas, astray. The resolution of the problem was for all to come into line with the decision made at a special meeting in Jerusalem (see Acts 15). There Paul, Barnabas and Peter recounted how the gentiles had come to conversion. With their input and discussion with the apostles and elders, James, as Jerusalem leader, concluded that circumcision was not to be imposed on adult gentile converts.

That Peter was reconciled with Paul is obvious here. Their relationship was clearly a brotherly one. It was a relationship that survived the human characteristics each man had. At the end of his life, Peter could refer to his colleague as "our beloved brother Paul" (2 Peter 3:15). There are other references to Peter in Paul's writings that show their friendship (see 1 Corinthians 1:12; 3:22). Paul also makes an interesting aside that confirms Cephas's marital status. He says, "Do we not have the right to take along a believing wife, as do the other apostles and the brothers of the Lord and Cephas?" (1 Corinthians 9:5).

In John's Gospel, we read that Christ put Peter to the test with an exchange that upset him (John 21:15–17). In a postresurrection appearance, Jesus asked him about the quality of his devotion: "Simon, son of John, do you love me more than these?" Then twice more, "Simon, son of John, do you love me?" When twice Peter replied, "Yes, Lord; you know that I love you," Jesus commanded, "Feed my lambs" and "Tend my sheep." John notes that "Peter was grieved because he said to him the third time, 'Do you love me?' and he said to him, 'Lord, you know everything; you know that I love you.' Jesus said to him, 'Feed my sheep.'" Peter learned a profound lesson in this exchange, one that would be tested as time went by in the Church's expansion. Further, Jesus told him that his life in caring for the sheep would not be easy and in fact that he would pay the ultimate price—with his life: "'When you are old, you will stretch out your hands, and another will dress you and carry you where you do not want to go.' (This he said to show by what kind of death he was to glorify God.) And after saying this he said to him, 'Follow me'" (verses 18–19). Like Jesus, Peter would end his life in martyrdom.

And here is an important point to understand. If we want to be true followers of Christ, we must do so as He desires, not according to our own agendas. Peter had to learn that.

The Apostle's Letters

When we study the New Testament record for details regarding the latter part of Peter's life, we come to two significant letters by his name. Yet some have doubted that the letters are Peter's, and they advance several arguments to support this idea. None are compelling, however. With respect to the first letter, the *English Standard Version Study Bible* outlines the arguments and the answers.

One objection is that a Galilean fisherman would not have written such good Greek. The answer is that Peter came from cross-cultural Galilee, where Greek was spoken. A second objection is that his theology sounds too much like Paul's. This is an amusing one, because often the case is made that the apostle to the Jews and the apostle to the gentiles had very different theologies. The answer to this objection is that it is not at all strange that two followers of Jesus should have the same beliefs. In fact, it's what would be expected. A further argument is that the Peter of the letters quotes the Septuagint, whereas the real Peter would have used the Hebrew Scriptures. But why wouldn't he use the Greek Old Testament when writing to Greek speakers? In a fourth objection, skeptics insist that Peter was already dead by the time the first letter was written, because they claim it reflects events in the Roman Empire at the end of the first century. But there is no internal evidence to support this speculation. Last, it's said that Peter does not refer to Jesus enough to demonstrate that he was the Peter who knew Him. Answer: This is a short letter for a specific purpose. That said, Peter does refer to Jesus' teachings, as we will see.

The first letter begins: "Peter, an apostle of Jesus Christ, to the pilgrims of the Dispersion in Pontus, Galatia, Cappadocia, Asia, and Bithynia, elect according to the foreknowledge of God the Father, in sanctification of the Spirit, for obedience and sprinkling of the blood of Jesus Christ: Grace to you and peace be multiplied" (1 Peter 1:1–2, NKJV).

The letter was probably written around the early 60s—in the reign of Emperor Nero—and is addressed to followers of Jesus in central and northern Asia Minor, just south of the Black Sea.

The letter opens in a similar way to James's epistle. It addresses believers who were predominantly gentile (though some Jews would likely have been included) in an area of the Diaspora where Jews had settled for at least two centuries after leaving their ancient homeland. One commentator says that Peter addressed his readers as if they were Jewish followers of Jesus. The order of the provinces listed is perhaps the way a courier would travel to them on an organized mail route.

Peter was setting down important foundational knowledge for believers. He was getting old and perhaps sensing that he had little time left (this becomes more apparent in the second letter), so he laid out fundamental truths to help everyone continue, despite difficulties. His emphasis and the emphasis of the grammatical structure in the opening verses is that it is not Peter who is important, but rather the called and chosen readers. He reminded them of the great calling given only to the few. He noted that this is the last age of man's rule now that Christ has come

(1 Peter 1:3–5). They were living in the space between the first and second comings. This belief is what helps sustain God's people when things get difficult in this world. When trials come, the hope of the future encourages them, and tests and trials are contextualized by the promise of Christ's second coming (1 Peter 1:6–9).

Peter knew that the follower of Jesus might sometimes diminish the value of these trials and tests. But he insisted that they are for our good—our learning—and that they benefit us eternally. The calling to be a follower is based on spiritual knowledge that God has progressively revealed. Our predecessors did not know what is now known following Christ's first coming. Peter explained that "the prophets who prophesied about the grace that was to be yours searched and inquired carefully, inquiring what person or time the Spirit of Christ in them was indicating when [it] predicted the sufferings of Christ and the subsequent glories. It was revealed to them that they were serving not themselves but you, in the things that have now been announced to you through those who preached the good news to you by the Holy Spirit sent from heaven, things into which angels long to look" (1 Peter 1:10–12).

The realization of this truth should lead to a mind that is convicted of the need to live a different life than the world around lives. Modern translators have expressed Peter's words as "preparing your minds for action" (1 Peter 1:13). The Greek verb underlying this means wrapping around the waist the long clothing of those times. A similar thought is found in Luke's Gospel, where Jesus uses a related verb to say, "Stay dressed for action and keep your lamps burning" (Luke 12:35). The verse in 1 Peter is one of the places where Jesus' teaching is apparent. Further, Peter reminds his readers of the goal of their conduct: "As obedient children, do not be conformed to the passions of your former ignorance, but as he who called you is holy, you also be holy in all your conduct, since it is written, "You shall be holy, for I am holy" (1 Peter 1:14–16).

One of the benefits of this knowledge is that believers can call on God the Father, the impartial judge. His Son's sacrifice means that whatever we do that is wrong in this life can be blotted out, if we seek God's forgiveness (1 Peter 1:17–21). Our purpose in doing this is to become more and more like the Father. To do so, we have to have our minds in gear.

An important byproduct of having God's Spirit at work in us is the ability to love brothers and sisters who are of the same mind. It also provides the important realization that this life is not all there is; in fact, it's nothing by comparison with our destiny, and this truth sustains us: "Since you have purified your souls in obeying the truth through the Spirit in sincere love of the brethren, love one another fervently with a pure heart, having been born again, not of corruptible seed but incorruptible, through the word of God which lives and abides forever, because 'All flesh is as grass, and all the glory of man as the flower of the grass. The grass withers, and its flower falls away, but the word of the Lord endures forever.' Now this is the word which by the gospel was preached to you" (1 Peter 1:22–25, NKJV).

God's Election

In chapter 2, Peter expands on the theme of interpersonal responsibility that he has introduced. He draws the conclusion that a person who is guided by God's Spirit will set aside the normal human tendencies to malign and deceive others (1 Peter 2:1–3). He had also recognized that Jesus is the living foundation stone for the house God is building from specially called and chosen human beings (1 Peter 2:4–5). This truth that God is not calling everyone in this life was something Peter gave voice to on the Day of Pentecost, following the coming of the Holy Spirit. He told the assembled crowd, "The promise is to you and to your children, and to all who are afar off, *as many as the Lord our God will call*" (Acts 2:39, NKJV, emphasis added). People cannot come to God unless He calls them. This is why Peter continues in his letter to the Church, "You are a chosen generation, a royal priesthood, a holy nation, His own special people, that you may proclaim the praises of Him who called you out of darkness into His marvelous light" (1 Peter 2:9, NKJV).

The remarkable change of heart that had come over those called out is the basis of Peter's appeal that they continue to live very different lives in respect of Christ's anticipated return, when other people will recognize their good works and give God the credit (verses 11–12).

This mode of expression is an indication of Peter's familiarity with Jesus' teaching. A similar thought is found in Matthew's Gospel, where Jesus is recorded as saying, "Let your light shine before others, so that they may see your good works and give glory to your Father who is in heaven" (Matthew 5:16).

In reality, Peter had not ceased to talk about Jesus' identity since the beginning of his own realization of whom he was dealing with. Jesus had asked the disciples, "'Who do people say that I am?' And they told him, 'John the Baptist; and others say, Elijah; and others, one of the prophets.'

And he asked them, "But who do you say that I am?' Peter answered him, 'You are the Christ'" (Mark 8:27–29).

Appreciation of the fact that God had sent His Son to show the way out of sin and the dilemma of human moral frailty led Peter to write a lengthy section in his first letter about a common problem and a common failing.

The common problem is mistreatment by humans around us. The common failing is unwillingness to be submissive to God in such circumstances. Peter cites several situations where the right thing to do is simply to be submissive and let time pass as a demonstration of faith that God will work everything out in His time.

Time Grows Short

Peter's first example concerns everyone's necessary submission to human government. In a first-century context he writes, "Be subject for the Lord's sake to every human institution, whether it be to the emperor as supreme, or to governors as sent by him to punish those who do evil and to praise those who do good. For this is the will of God, that by doing good you should put to silence the ignorance of foolish people. Live as people who are free, not using your freedom as a cover-up for evil, but living as servants of God. Honor everyone. Love the brotherhood. Fear God. Honor the emperor" (1 Peter 2:13–17).

Of course, this advice runs counter to the way of the world. Loyalty to a higher power whose ways are not our ways demands a different approach. Peter had demonstrated how that can be accomplished shortly after he and the other disciples received the Holy Spirit on the Day of Pentecost. The Jewish religious leaders had tried to prevent them from teaching about Jesus. In response, Peter and the other apostles had expressed the conviction that they "ought to obey God rather than men" (Acts 5:28–29, NKJV).

In his letter, Peter turns next to servants (slaves, in Roman times). What should a slave who was a follower of Jesus do in the difficult circumstance of serving an unconverted master? Today we might substitute the word *employee* for "servant" or "slave" and ask how a convert should relate to a boss who is unconverted. Peter instructs: "Servants, be subject to your masters with all respect, not only to the good and gentle but also to the unjust" (1 Peter 2:18).

The idea of continuing to work for someone who is unjust does not sit well in today's world, though Peter is not saying that there are no circumstances in which a servant should attempt to leave such employment. What he is saying is that followers of Jesus will try to do all in their power to serve well, despite employer opposition. After all, Jesus suffered greatly for doing right, and He is the follower's primary example (verse 21).

Peter cites Christ's physical suffering as the ultimate example of what may be endured to demonstrate commitment to doing things the right way. In a sense Jesus' followers have been called to endure suffering, should that be required to follow God's way. Some might wonder how much they should put up with. There are limits, of course. But first there will usually be a period of endurance while we wait for God's intervention.

Wives and Husbands

Peter's third area of discussion is the role of the wife whose husband is not a follower of Jesus. In a passage that sounds strangely archaic in the 21st century, he writes, "Wives, be subject to your own husbands" (1 Peter 3:1). In this long section on submission, Peter is actually dealing with social relationships in the ancient world—individuals and government, servants and masters, and now husbands and wives. He teaches that a wife must be submissive to her husband in his role of family leader. This is not about submission to autocratic and abusive men but rather submission with the goal of family harmony.

It is possible that the godly wife's right behavior may in fact persuade her husband that following the way of God is beneficial. Peter's instruction also includes appropriate forms of dress and grooming for such women (verses 3–4). Not conforming to the world around means not following every fad and fashion, yet at the same time not looking like a misfit. It's about a balanced, middle-of-the-road approach. Peter also emphasizes that women give priority to caring for the inner self and develop "the imperishable beauty of a gentle and quiet spirit" (verse 4) over outward beauty.

In his instruction to husbands who are believers, Peter begins with the word *likewise*. The word is easily passed over; but Peter means "in the same way as wives," as regards submission. Husbands have to live with wives according to understanding: How does a woman function? What are her needs? How do they differ from the man's needs? If he is to be an effective husband, he is required to step outside his comfort zone and submit to his wife's needs and recognize that there is an equally valid way of viewing situations that may be foreign to a man: "Likewise, husbands, live with your wives in an understanding way, showing honor to the woman as the weaker vessel, since they are heirs with you of the grace of life, so that your prayers may not be hindered" (verse 7).

Mutual Respect

Peter's fifth example includes everyone once again, but this time not in the context of submission to government but to each other: "Finally, all of you, have unity of mind, sympathy, brotherly love, a tender heart, and a humble mind" (verse 8). He reminds his audience that revenge, or countering evil with evil, is not God's way. Better to bless than revile, to avoid practicing deceit, and to seek peace with others. That way guarantees God's willingness to see and hear us (verses 9–12).

Again, this is a very different Peter than the one who wondered in his earlier life what he would get for his devotion to Jesus' cause: "We have left everything and followed you. What then will we have?" (Matthew 19:27). Or the younger Peter, who engaged in vigorous debate about who among the disciples would be the greatest (Mark 9:33–34).

Peter had learned that there is a submissive way of dealing with life's many circumstances. It is harmless and brings only good results, even when we suffer for doing what is right (1 Peter 3:13–14). And here is another echo of Jesus' teaching. Peter had heard Jesus say, "Blessed are those who are persecuted for righteousness' sake, for theirs is the kingdom of heaven" (Matthew 5:10).

In his letter he continues with the reminder that Jesus' followers must not be afraid of opposition; rather, he instructs, "always [be] prepared to make a defense to anyone who asks you for a reason for the hope that is in you; yet do it with gentleness and respect, having a good conscience, so that, when you are slandered, those who revile your good behavior in Christ may be put to shame. For it is better to suffer for doing good, if that should be God's will, than for doing evil" (1 Peter 3:15–17).

The true followers of Jesus are to be prepared to patiently struggle at times. That may mean not going along with the world around and its pressures to conform. Peter's readers had formerly experienced a different way of life—"living in sensuality, passions, drunkenness, orgies, drinking parties, and lawless idolatry." Now that they no longer joined in, their former friends were surprised and then angry (1 Peter 4:3–4).

But the people of God must behave differently than others around, especially in light of their time in history: "The end of all things is at hand; therefore be self-controlled and sober-minded for the sake of your prayers" (verse 7). This does not mean that it will always be easy to live as a follower of Jesus. Peter warns that they should anticipate times of the testing of their faith: "Do not be surprised at the fiery trial when it comes upon you to test you, as though something strange were happening to you" (verse 12). If any suffer as followers of Christ, they should rather rejoice that they are sharing in Christ's own sufferings and will be blessed accordingly (verses 13–19).

Peter the Shepherd

What Jesus said to Peter in one of their last encounters now returns as a theme. Peter was told, "Feed my sheep" (John 21). That is to say, in effect, "Take care of my followers." In the concluding part of his letter, Peter explains how this is to be accomplished by truly caring ministers: "Exercis[e] oversight, not under compulsion, but willingly, as God would have you; not for shameful gain, but eagerly; not domineering over those in your charge, but being examples to the flock. And when the chief Shepherd appears, you will receive the unfading crown of glory" (1 Peter 5:2–4).

Returning to the essentials of humility and mutual submission as keys to right living in God's sight, he says this to those who are in the care of the ministry: "You who are younger, be subject to the elders. Clothe yourselves, all of you, with humility toward one another, for 'God opposes the proud but gives grace to the humble.' Humble yourselves, therefore, under the mighty hand of God so that at the proper time he may exalt you, casting all your anxieties on him, because he cares for you" (verses 5–7).

Recall that Peter is the same person who fell into Satan's traps at times. Now he has come to understand the importance of resisting him. We know that Jesus rebuked Peter for allowing Satan to influence his thinking: "Get behind me, Satan! You are a hindrance to me. For you are not setting your mind on the things of God, but on the things of man" (Matthew 16:23). He had also warned Peter that Satan was actively against him: "Simon, Simon, behold, Satan demanded to have you, that he might sift you like wheat" (Luke 22:31).

Now, near the end of his life, Peter is able to say: "Be sober-minded; be watchful. Your adversary the devil prowls around like a roaring lion, seeking someone to devour. Resist him, firm in your faith . . ." (1 Peter 5:8–9).

Peter made great progress in his own spiritual journey. Suffering for following Christ's way and submission to God's will, as well as faith in the eventual positive outcome of a life lived under God's guiding hand, are all acknowledged in this marvelous product of a mature mind: "After you have suffered a little while, the God of all grace, who has called you to his eternal glory in Christ, will himself restore, confirm, strengthen, and establish you. To him be the dominion forever and ever. Amen" (verses 10–11).

Chapter Nine

What Kind of People Should You Be?

"We have the prophetic word confirmed, which you do well to heed as a light that shines in a dark place, until the day dawns and the morning star rises in your hearts."

As the apostle Peter began his second (and for us, final) letter, he was nearing the end of his eventful life as a follower of Jesus.

What was most important for him at this stage was to motivate his audience and make it possible for them to remember the way of life he had lived: "I think it right, as long as I am in this body, to stir you up by way of reminder, since I know that the putting off of my body will be soon, as our Lord Jesus Christ made clear to me. And I will make every effort so that after my departure you may be able at any time to recall these things" (2 Peter 1:13–15).

This was especially important, because teachers who taught falsely about Jesus had become a major problem and were traveling across large parts of the Roman world.

Opening Thoughts

The letter opens with the greeting, "Simeon Peter, a servant and apostle of Jesus Christ . . ." (verse 1a). While Peter refers to himself as an apostle, he is first a bondservant. The Greek word *doulos* means not merely a servant but a slave. It signifies someone who is completely given over to the authority of another. So Peter is *under* authority to Christ as a slave; and as an apostle (in Greek, *apostolos*, "he that is sent"), he *possesses* authority from Christ as one He has sent out.

Peter continues with the recognition that he is writing to people with whom he shares equality in God's sight. Though he is one of the apostles, he is no different in terms of his faith than his brothers and sisters: ". . . to those who have obtained a faith of equal standing with ours by the righteousness of our God and Savior Jesus Christ" (verse 1b).

Peter and the other apostles shared the privilege of seeing Jesus firsthand, but his audience is not to be looked down on because they were not equally eyewitnesses. A similar thought is found in John's Gospel when Jesus says to the doubting apostle Thomas, "Have you believed because you have seen me? Blessed are those who have not seen and yet have believed" (John 20:29). Belief is what is fundamental, not how it originated.

Peter wants his audience to have the blessing of peace and knowledge of God and Christ. He reminds them that God, by His power, has granted not only "all things that pertain to life and godliness" but also "precious and very great promises, so that through them you may become partakers of the divine nature, having escaped from the corruption [depravity] that is in the world because of sinful desire" (2 Peter 1:3–4). It is because of God's involvement in their lives and their rejection of the world's way of behaving that they have the possibility of taking on God's own nature.

God's calling is the reason Peter mentions next the need for constant development of several personal characteristics. He writes: "Make every effort to supplement your faith with virtue, and virtue with knowledge, and knowledge with self-control, and self-control with steadfastness, and steadfastness with godliness, and godliness with brotherly affection, and brotherly affection with love" (verses 5–7). If the members of the Church will do these things, they will not fail to produce good spiritual fruit in their lives and will avoid the spiritual blindness that can result from failure to continuously improve. They will then accomplish the goal of entering God's future world (verses 8–11).

The Kingdom to Come

Peter is confirming what he long believed and taught—that there will be a kingdom of God *on the earth*. The basis for his belief is in part that he saw Jesus in a resurrected state. But there is more. He refers next to an extraordinary experience, one he could never have forgotten. It gave him a glimpse of the future God has planned. Not only did he experience the effect of resurrection in the case of Jesus, he previewed aspects of the kingdom to come and heard God's voice confirm it. He says that because of this kind of experience, his witness is true. He saw it for himself, and his word can be trusted. It's not that he and his fellow disciples followed speculations and ideas that had no substance—rather like in our day when people talk about "spirituality," yet it is vague and has no firm basis. Peter reminds his readers that the knowledge they share is based on solid fact. He writes, "We did not follow cleverly devised myths when we made known to you the power and coming of our Lord Jesus Christ, but we were eyewitnesses of his majesty. For when he received honor and glory from God the Father, and the voice was borne to him by the Majestic Glory, 'This is my beloved Son, with whom I am well pleased,' we ourselves heard this very voice borne from heaven, for we were with him on the holy mountain" (verses 16–18).

This, of course, is a reference to the much earlier experience of transfiguration, when Peter and two others saw a vision of the resurrected Jesus in the kingdom of God (see Matthew 16:24–17:9). It confirmed Jesus as the Messiah, the Anointed One who was to come. Peter would later recall this event and begin to understand in a much deeper way what it signified. For him it was further evidence that the prophecies about the coming of the Messiah had been fulfilled in Jesus.

As Peter says in his final letter, "We have the prophetic word confirmed, which you do well to heed as a light that shines in a dark place, until the day dawns and the morning star rises in your hearts; knowing this first, that no prophecy of Scripture is of any private interpretation [or origin], for prophecy never came by the will of man, but holy men of God spoke as they were moved by the Holy Spirit" (2 Peter 1:19–21, NKJV).

Peter makes some very important points here. Prophecies about Christ's first coming have been fulfilled, and Peter is a witness to that. He taught this much earlier in his ministry. And just as surely as they have been fulfilled in respect of the first coming, so there are prophecies about the second coming that will come to pass (see Acts 3:18–21). At the moment, they are like a light shining in a dark place for those who understand. As the day of Christ's return gets closer, they will shine more brightly (become more evident or understandable), until that growing light culminates in His second coming (see Matthew 24:30).

Another important point in this passage is the simple, logical fact that God's prophetic statements do not originate in human minds. What Peter writes here is not a statement about the *interpretation* of prophecy; it's about its origin. The source of these prophecies about Christ is God. Humans inspired by the Holy Spirit (the mind of God) wrote them down. But they are not of human origin. That's to say they can be trusted implicitly, unlike human prophecies.

Beware False Teachers

Perhaps with this difference between God's foretelling and human prediction in mind, Peter next warns of the dangers of listening to false teachers who inevitably come around from time to time. They exploit people's weaknesses, doubts and fears. It has always been so, and Peter reminds his readers that the children of Israel suffered the same difficulties. Such people "will secretly bring in destructive heresies, even denying the Lord who bought them, and bring on themselves swift destruction." Their "destructive ways" cause "the way of truth [to] be blasphemed" (2 Peter 2:1–2, NKJV).

The "way of truth" is God's way of life. Peter explains the mentality and fate of people who decide to go the opposite way and assures his audience that God will deal with such people as He has in the past. This has included sinning angels, the pre-Flood population of Noah's time, and the inhabitants of Sodom and Gomorrah—all of whom are examples for anyone who would live in an ungodly way (verses 4–7).

Peter had plainly had enough of dealing with people who had gone wrong. It's interesting how quickly the mind becomes disrespectful of the authority that God has given His servants (verse 10), once there is a turning away to the authority of self. When the mind becomes opposed to God's servants, depravity sets in.

What Peter has to say next about false teachers is shocking in our world, which prizes political correctness. He does not hold back: "These, like irrational animals, creatures of instinct, born to be caught and destroyed, blaspheming about matters of which they are ignorant, will also be destroyed in their destruction. . . . They are blots and blemishes, reveling in their deceptions, while they feast with you. They have eyes full of adultery, insatiable for sin. They entice unsteady souls. They have hearts trained in greed.

Accursed children! Forsaking the right way, they have gone astray. . . . These are waterless springs and mists driven by a storm. For them the gloom of utter darkness has been reserved" (verses 12–15, 17).

The way that false teachers go about their deceptive business is laid out. These are things to be aware of: "For, speaking loud boasts of folly, they entice by sensual passions of the flesh those who are barely escaping from those who live in error. They promise them freedom, but they themselves are slaves of corruption. For whatever overcomes a person, to that he is enslaved" (verses 18–19).

Peter's conclusion about those who have been enlightened and subsequently heeded false teachers is delivered with strong imagery: "For it would have been better for them never to have known the way of righteousness than after knowing it to turn back from the holy commandment delivered to them. What the true proverb says, has happened to them: 'The dog returns to its own vomit, and the sow, after washing herself, returns to wallow in the mire'" (verses 21–22).

In the Last Days

In chapter 3, Peter turns again to the purpose of both letters: "This is now the second letter that I am writing to you, beloved. In both of them I am stirring up your sincere mind by way of reminder, that you should remember the predictions [prophecies] of the holy prophets and the commandment of the Lord and Savior through your apostles." Recalling for his readers their calling in the context of a world of opposition to God's way and denial of Christ's return, he writes, "Scoffers will come in the last days with scoffing, following their own sinful desires. They will say, 'Where is the promise of his coming? For ever since the fathers fell asleep, all things are continuing as they were from the beginning of creation'" (verses 1–4).

This sounds very familiar in today's English-speaking world, which is experiencing a major attack from educated atheists. But as Peter says of those in his day, "they deliberately overlook this fact, that the heavens existed long ago, and the earth was formed out of water and through water by the word of God, and that by means of these the world that then existed was deluged with water and perished. But by the same word the heavens and earth that now exist are stored up for fire, being kept until the day of judgment and destruction of the ungodly" (verses 5–7).

Peter then reminds his readers that the temptation to think that because nothing like this has happened for thousands of years, therefore nothing will, is foolish: "Do not overlook this one fact, beloved, that with the Lord one day is as a thousand years, and a thousand years as one day" (verse 8). The delay results from His patience with us and His desire that all will come to fully accept His way in a repentant frame of mind. God will keep His word: "The Lord is not slow to fulfill his promise as some count slowness, but is patient toward you, not wishing that any should perish, but that all should reach repentance" (verse 9).

Getting humans to see the need to repent, and then do it and live that right way, is very difficult. The hardest thing for a human to do is admit he or she is wrong. The next most difficult is to change and practice the right way.

In this context, Peter writes about the day of God's intervention that is yet ahead. This is something that the early Church firmly believed. It is found in the Gospels, in Paul's letters, and in the writings of the other apostles. It is an event that will catch most by surprise: "The day of the Lord will come like a thief, and then the heavens will pass away with a roar, and the heavenly bodies will be burned up and dissolved, and the earth and the works that are done on it will be exposed" (verse 10).

An important question for the Church springs from knowing God's coming judgment of human ways. It concerns the kind of spiritual progress God's people should be making. Peter is passing on knowledge that should make a difference in how life is lived: "Since all these things are thus to be dissolved, what sort of people ought you to be in lives of holiness and godliness, waiting for and hastening the coming of the day of God, because of which the heavens will be set on fire and dissolved, and the heavenly bodies will melt as they burn! But according to his promise we are waiting for new heavens and a new earth in which righteousness dwells" (verses 11–13).

Last Words

Peter's concluding remarks—the last the Church had in writing by this leader from its earliest days, one who had been with Christ and had witnessed so much, struggled so much and achieved so much personally and collectively—are about persistence in holding on to the values of God and growing in all that Jesus Christ represented: "Beloved, since you are waiting for these [new heavens and earth], be diligent to be found by him without spot or blemish, and at peace. And count the patience of our Lord as salvation. . . . Knowing this beforehand, take care that you are not carried away with the error of lawless people and lose your own stability. But grow in the grace and knowledge of our Lord and Savior Jesus Christ. To him be the glory both now and to the day of eternity. Amen" (verses 14–15, 17–18).

Jude's Letter

A New Testament letter that is often read side by side with 2 Peter is by Jude. In fact, one could be forgiven for thinking that one writer had copied the other. There are many overlapping concepts and linguistic expressions, especially concerning those who come with false teaching (see Jude 4–13, 16–19, and 2 Peter 2:1–18; 3:1–3). It may be that Peter read Jude's letter before writing his own for a different purpose.

Jude says he is the brother of James (verse 1), who was very likely "the Lord's brother" (Galatians 1:19), leader of the Jerusalem church and author of the New Testament book of James. In other words, like James, Jude was one of the other sons of Joseph and Mary (see Matthew 13:55; Mark 6:3).

His concern in writing his short, 25-verse letter is to encourage the called-out members of the Church to stay true to "the faith that was once for all delivered to the saints" (Jude 3). Like Peter, he had been confronted by false teachers who had surreptitiously invaded the Church and brought with them spurious doctrines and sinful practices. Their emphasis on sensuality was a perversion of God's grace and a denial of Christ's way (verse 4).

Using Old Testament examples, Jude reminds the Church that God acted against any unbelievers among those who left Egypt in the Exodus; against angels who failed in their responsibilities in the pre-Adamic world on the earth; and against sinning cities such as Sodom and Gomorrah (verses 5–7).

False teachers behave like those whom God punished in the past. They commit the same kinds of sin through self-reliance, rejection of authority over them, and blasphemy. In dispute with the devil, even the archangel Michael did not pronounce a blasphemous judgment on Satan, rather holding back and allowing God to be the judge (verse 9). False teachers are like animals without capacity to reason, with only the ability to act instinctively. Jude says that such people have committed a combination of sins, exemplified individually by Cain, the first murderer; Balaam, the false prophet; and Korah, the leader of a rebellion against Moses (verse 11). Among God's people, such men are "hidden reefs at your love feasts, as they feast with you without fear, shepherds feeding themselves; waterless clouds, swept along by winds; fruitless trees in late autumn, twice dead, uprooted; wild waves of the sea, casting up the foam of their own shame; wandering stars, for whom the gloom of utter darkness has been reserved forever" (verses 12–13).

Jude says that the righteous Enoch, the seventh generation from Adam, spoke a prophecy about the end of such men. They will be judged by the returning Christ and His saints. False teachers are "grumblers, malcontents, following their own sinful desires; they are loud-mouthed boasters, showing favoritism to gain advantage" (verse 16).

Jude concludes his letter of warning and encouragement by reminding the Church of the prophetic expressions of the apostles. They said that this world of human development will produce people with scoffing attitudes. Such individuals will cause division, being worldly in their thinking and devoid of God's Spirit (verses 17–19). God's people must simply keep going down the path that leads to eternal life, not being dissuaded. They are to do what they can to help brothers and sisters who may be caught up in error, caused by doubt and indulgence in the world's ways. God will preserve His people through all difficulties, and Jude's prayer is that they will be brought "blameless before the presence of his glory with great joy." He concludes, "To the only God, our Savior, through Jesus Christ our Lord, be glory, majesty, dominion, and authority, before all time and now and forever. Amen" (verses 24–25).

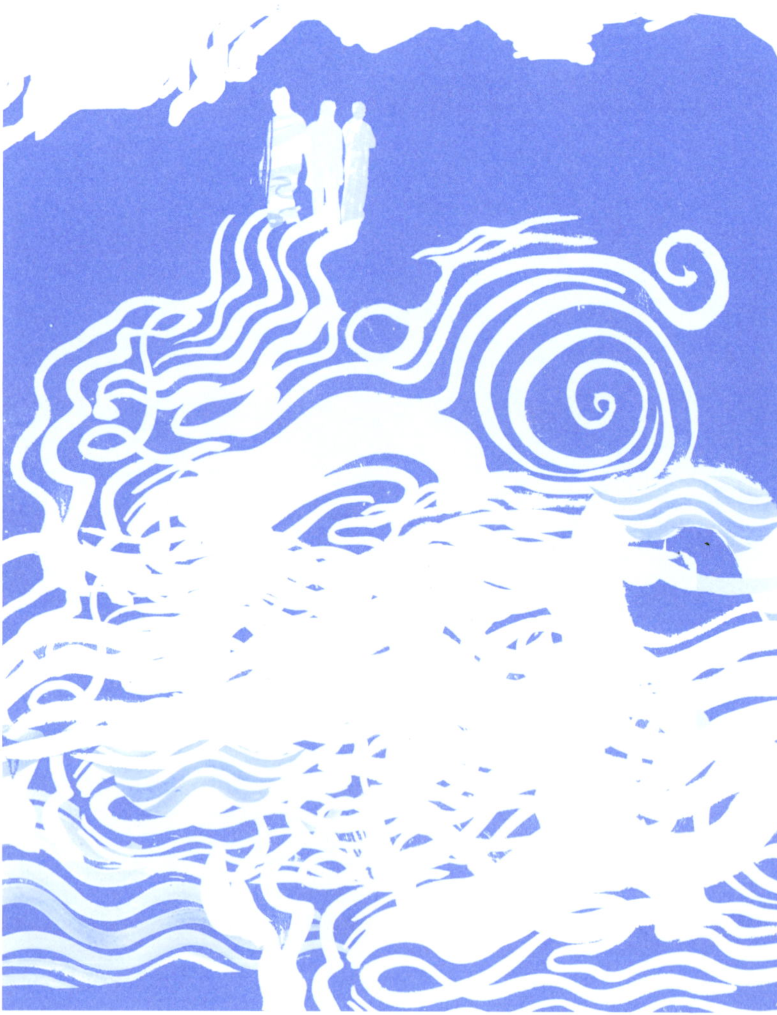

Son of Thunder

"Follow me, and I will make you fishers of men."

The last surviving apostle was John. By the end of the tumultuous first century, John had experienced all the joys and disappointments of life as a follower of Jesus. He had been there from the start of Jesus' ministry, had witnessed the transfiguration of his Teacher, and knew who Jesus was. He had seen thousands of people come into the newly formed New Testament Church—three thousand in one day, and five thousand shortly thereafter. And he had cared for Jesus' mother Mary, perhaps taking her with him to Ephesus.

John had also wrestled with the growing spread of Gnostic ideas. A so-called fellow minister had even prevented him from teaching. He had been held captive on Patmos, a Roman prison island. And while there in the middle of the 90s C.E., by which time he was quite old, he received the overwhelming series of visions known as the Apocalypse, or Revelation.

All of this happened over a period of about 70 years. It is thought that John lived into the reign of the emperor Trajan (98–117).

As noted, Ephesus apparently became his base after the departure of the Church from Jerusalem in the late 60s as they fled from the advancing Romans. The *Anchor-Yale Bible Dictionary* notes: "The common tradition of the church affirmed that, after his leadership role in the church of Jerusalem, John moved to Ephesus, where he lived to an old age and died a natural death. The tradition is summarized by Eusebius."

Church historian Eusebius of Caesarea, who wrote in the late third and early fourth century, often quoted earlier writers whose works are in some cases no longer extant. He mentioned a few of them as supporters of the tradition that

John lived in Ephesus, that he worked there, and that he was alive at the end of the first century. One of his sources was Irenaeus (ca. 130–202), whose works are still in existence. Irenaeus claims he got reports about John's ministry in Ephesus from Papias (ca. 60–130) and Polycarp (ca. 70–156), whose lives overlapped with John's. Polycarp was in fact a disciple of John. Others also testified to John's ministry in Ephesus, though pertinent texts exist only to the extent that later writers such as Eusebius quoted them.

Sons of Thunder

In the Bible the apostle John is mentioned by name 30 times—in Matthew, Mark, Luke, Acts and Galatians. We are first introduced to him in the book of Matthew: "While walking by the Sea of Galilee, [Jesus] saw two brothers, Simon (who is called Peter) and Andrew his brother, casting a net into the sea, for they were fishermen. And he said to them, 'Follow me, and I will make you fishers of men.' Immediately they left their nets and followed him. And going on from there he saw two other brothers, James the son of Zebedee and John his brother, in the boat with Zebedee their father, mending their nets, and he called them. Immediately they left the boat and their father and followed him" (Matthew 4:18–22).

Here we are introduced to John as the brother of James, both of them sons of Zebedee. Their mother, it appears, was a follower of Jesus and was present at the crucifixion. (Perhaps she was one of those women who helped Him when He was in Galilee; based on references in Mark 15:40 and Matthew 27:56, her name may have been Salome.) When the brothers left their father to follow

Jesus, hired hands remained to help him in his fishing business. The fact that the family had enough money to hire servants suggests that it was probably a reasonably successful business (Mark 1:20).

In Mark's Gospel we also learn that just as Jesus renamed Simon, He also gave these brothers a special name: "And he went up on the mountain and called to him those whom he desired, and they came to him. And he appointed twelve (whom he also named apostles) so that they might be with him and he might send them out to preach and have authority to cast out demons. He appointed the twelve: Simon (to whom he gave the name Peter); James the son of Zebedee and John the brother of James (to whom he gave the name Boanerges, that is, Sons of Thunder) . . ." (Mark 3:13–17).

Perhaps this is a clue to their nature. Three examples show why Jesus might have given them this name, each of which provided opportunities to teach certain principles. These experiences undoubtedly affected John, who did not write the books we have until near the end of the first century. By the time he set them down, he was a very mature person. Earlier in life, he seems a rather different man.

Three Examples

At a certain point in Jesus' ministry, "John said to him, 'Teacher, we saw someone casting out demons in your name, and we tried to stop him, because he was not following us.' But Jesus said, 'Do not stop him, for no one who does a mighty work in my name will be able soon afterward to speak evil of me. For the one who is not against us is for us. For truly, I say to you, whoever gives you a cup of water to drink because you belong to Christ will by no means lose his reward'" (Mark 9:38–41).

Here Jesus spoke to having a more measured approach to life's events—not getting immediately overexcited about things that happen. It doesn't say that Christ considered everyone who did things in His name to represent Him, or to be equal in any sense. Many people misunderstand this scripture, thinking it means that everyone's work is equally valid as long as they use the name of Christ. But Jesus didn't say that. He just said, in effect, "Relax, don't get too excited about it. If that's what they're doing, as long as they're not opposing us, then that's fine." He didn't say, "We're all the same" or "Go join them." He simply said, "Leave them alone."

In a second example, Mark relates that "James and John, the sons of Zebedee, came up to him and said to him, 'Teacher, we want you to do for us whatever we ask of you'" (Mark 10:35). That's quite a statement. "Why don't you just do everything we want?"

"And he said to them, 'What do you want me to do for you?' And they said to him, 'Grant us to sit, one at your right hand and one at your left, in your glory'" (verses 36–37).

This is presumption in the extreme—naked ambition. Jesus used the opportunity to teach humility, not behaving as many leaders in the world behave, not ruling as many human beings rule. "[He] said to them, 'You do not know what you are asking. . . . To sit at my right hand or at my left is not mine to grant, but it is for those for whom it has been prepared. And when the ten heard it, they began to be indignant at James and John. And Jesus called them to him and said to them, 'You know that those who are considered rulers of the Gentiles lord it over them, and their great ones exercise authority over them. But it shall not be so among you. But whoever would be great among you must be your servant, and whoever would be first among you must be slave of all. For even the Son of Man came not to be served but to serve, and to give his life as a ransom for many'" (verses 38–45).

By now the brothers had been with Jesus for about three years. But what was their state of mind?

Here's the third example, which perhaps best illustrates the aptness of the title Jesus gave them: "When the days drew near for him to be taken up, he set his face to go to Jerusalem. And he sent messengers ahead of him, who went and entered a village of the Samaritans, to make preparations for him. But the people did not receive him, because his face was set toward Jerusalem. And when his disciples James and John saw it, they said, 'Lord, do you want us to tell fire to come down from heaven and consume them?' But he turned and rebuked them. And they went on to another village" (Luke 9:51–56).

Despite this strong, demanding, fiery, impetuous aspect of the brothers' nature, John was later known not as a "son of thunder," but as the "apostle of love" for his promotion of outgoing love as a godly attribute. As we saw in Peter's case, this is an indication of how much a person can change under God's guidance.

A Developing Leader

As they matured, the two brothers were singled out for an important role. The naming of James and John early in the list of disciples (Matthew 10:2–3) reflects in part the chronological order of their calling, but it's also an indication of their eventual leadership based on their experiences from the beginning of Jesus' ministry.

For example, they were present when He performed an early miracle. Jesus "left the synagogue and entered the house of Simon and Andrew, with James and John. Now Simon's mother-in-law lay ill with a fever, and immediately they told him about her. And he came and took her by the hand and lifted her up, and the fever left her, and she began to serve them" (Mark 1:29–31).

The two brothers were also among the few allowed to be present at the raising of Jairus's daughter (Jairus was a local synagogue leader): "Someone from the ruler's house came and said, 'Your daughter is dead; do not trouble the Teacher any more.' But Jesus on hearing this answered him, 'Do not fear; only believe, and she will be well.' And when he came to the house, he allowed no one to enter with him, except Peter and John and James, and the father and mother of the child. . . . Taking her by the hand he called, saying, 'Child, arise.' And her spirit returned, and she got up at once" (Luke 8:49–55).

Later, James and John accompanied Jesus up a mountain and saw a vision of their Master in the kingdom of God: "And after six days Jesus took with him Peter and James, and John his brother, and led them up a high mountain by themselves. And he was transfigured before them, and his face shone like the sun, and his clothes became white as light" (Matthew 17:1–2). John saw it and was convicted, and this became an important aspect of his biography.

Further, according to Mark, Jesus' explanation of the end of the age was directed to James, John and two others:

"And as he sat on the Mount of Olives opposite the temple, Peter and James and John and Andrew asked him privately, 'Tell us, when will these things be, and what will be the sign when all these things are about to be accomplished?'" (Mark 13:3–4).

And again, when the time came for the final Passover meal, John was one of two disciples sent to prepare it: "Then came the day of Unleavened Bread [that is, the start of the Passover season], on which the Passover lamb had to be sacrificed. So Jesus sent Peter and John, saying, 'Go and prepare the Passover for us, that we may eat it'" (Luke 22:7–8).

Finally, during Jesus' most intense time in the Garden of Gethsemane, "he took with him Peter and James and John, and began to be greatly distressed and troubled" (Mark 14:33).

John's Growing Presence

John is not mentioned again in the three synoptic Gospels as they go on to relate Jesus' death and resurrection. And the Gospel of John doesn't mention him at all, at least not directly.

But he is named again at the beginning of the book of Acts: "Then they returned to Jerusalem from the mount called Olivet, which is near Jerusalem, a Sabbath day's journey away. And when they had entered, they went up to the upper room, where they were staying, Peter and John and James and Andrew, Philip and Thomas, Bartholomew and Matthew. . . . All these with one accord were devoting themselves to prayer, together with the women and Mary the mother of Jesus, and his brothers" (Acts 1:12–14).

Note that John, who had been asked by Jesus to take care of His mother (John 19:26–27), now takes precedence over James—an indication of his developing role.

By this time John is often linked with Peter, and this continues through the early chapters of Acts: "Now Peter and John were going up to the temple at the hour of prayer, the ninth hour. And a man lame from birth . . . fixed his attention on them, expecting to receive something from them. But Peter said, 'I have no silver and gold, but what I do have I give to you. In the name of Jesus Christ of Nazareth, rise up and walk!' And he took him by the right hand and raised him up. . . . While he clung to Peter and John, all the people, utterly astounded, ran together to them in the portico called Solomon's" (Acts 3:1–11).

Peter explained to them how all of this had happened. The account in Acts says that John was also involved in the speaking, and that their speech attracted the attention of the religious leaders: "And as they were speaking to the people, the priests and the captain of the temple and the Sadducees came upon them, greatly annoyed because they were teaching the people and proclaiming in Jesus the resurrection from the dead. And they arrested them and put them in custody until the next day, for it was already evening. But many of those who had heard the word believed, and the number of the men came to about five thousand. On the next day their rulers and elders and scribes gathered together in Jerusalem. . . . And when they had set them in the midst, they inquired, 'By what power or by what name did you do this?'" (Acts 4:1–7).

Peter told them how it happened and who Jesus was. Though Peter is credited with speaking, it was the courage of both men that took the religious leaders aback: "Now when they saw the boldness of Peter and John, and perceived that they were uneducated, common men, they were astonished. And they recognized that they had been with Jesus" (verse 13).

Unable to act against the two men, the religious leaders had to let them go. "When they were released, they went to their friends and reported what the chief priests and the elders had said to them. And when they heard it, they lifted their voices together to God. . . . When they had prayed, the place in which they were gathered together was shaken, and they were all filled with the Holy Spirit and continued to speak the word of God with boldness" (verses 23–31).

This was yet another experience that informed John's ongoing ministry.

Further Growth

John's role continued to grow as the young Church increased. When the gospel went out to the region north of Judea through Philip, and "the apostles at Jerusalem heard that Samaria had received the word of God, they sent to them Peter and John, who came down and prayed for them that they might receive the Holy Spirit, for [it] had not yet fallen on any of them, but they had only been baptized in the name of the Lord Jesus" (Acts 8:14–16).

One of those baptized was Simon Magus. But the magician, who was involved with incipient Gnosticism, had ulterior motives. John was present when Peter severely rebuked the false teacher (verses 17–23). This was a significant event, for John later had to deal with Gnostic influences within the Church.

In time John was mentioned by Paul as one of three leaders in Jerusalem following Christ's death and resurrection. Paul wrote: "When they saw that I had been entrusted with the gospel to the uncircumcised, just as Peter had been entrusted with the gospel to the circumcised (for he who worked through Peter for his apostolic ministry to the circumcised worked also through me for mine to the Gentiles), and when James [the brother of Jesus] and Cephas and John, who seemed to be pillars, perceived the grace that was given to me, they gave the right hand of fellowship to Barnabas and me, that we should go to the Gentiles and they to the circumcised" (Galatians 2:7–9).

Apostle of Love

"Whoever hates his brother is in the darkness and walks in the darkness, and does not know where he is going, because the darkness has blinded his eyes."

Though Jesus had named John a Son of Thunder, as his life progressed, he became better described as the apostle of love.

This is evident in the New Testament writings that bear his name or that are attributed to him by conservative scholars. This includes the Gospel of John, his three pastoral letters and the book of Revelation. Not every commentary agrees that John wrote everything that appears under or is associated with his name. Some question his authorship of the Gospel; others doubt that he wrote the letters; still others balk at his involvement with the book of Revelation. Many conservative scholars agree, though, that there is sufficient internal evidence, cross-referencing and weight of tradition to be reasonably sure that John wrote all of them. There is also general agreement among such scholars that John wrote late in the first century, after everything else that comprises the New Testament was written. This is the position taken here.

Evidence of the Author

One of the evidences of John's authorship of the Gospel is oddly that it contains no direct reference to him by name. That's not to say he doesn't appear; he is indicated at the end of the book, when following Jesus' death, some of the disciples have gone back to fishing. John writes, "After this Jesus revealed himself again to the disciples by the Sea of Tiberias, and he revealed himself in this way" (John 21:1). This is an important phrase—"he revealed Himself in this way." What is about to happen is a miraculous catch of fish that parallels the account of the fishermen's convincing early encounter with Jesus (see Luke 5:1–11). Was this the incident that came to John's mind in the events described in John 21? This may be a clue to why Jesus revealed himself to them in this way by the Sea of Galilee following the resurrection.

John writes, "Just as day was breaking, Jesus stood on the shore; yet the disciples did not know that it was Jesus. Jesus said to them, 'Children, do you have any fish?' They answered him, 'No.' He said to them, 'Cast the net on the right side of the boat, and you will find some.' So they cast it, and now they were not able to haul it in because of the quantity of fish. That disciple whom Jesus loved therefore said to Peter, 'It is the Lord!'" (John 21:4–7). John no doubt recalled the parallel earlier incident. The phrase "that disciple whom Jesus loved"—or similar wording—occurs several times in the latter part of the Gospel and has been understood to be John's way of referring to himself (see John 13:23; 19:26).

The description of what happened when Jesus' body went missing also involved "the disciple whom Jesus loved": "Now on the first day of the week Mary Magdalene came to the tomb early, while it was still dark, and saw that the stone had been taken away from the tomb. So she ran and went to Simon Peter and the other disciple, the one whom Jesus loved, and said to them, 'They have taken the Lord out of the tomb, and we do not know where they have laid him.' So Peter went out with the other disciple, and they were going toward the tomb. Both of them were running together, but the other disciple outran Peter and reached the tomb first. And stooping to look in, he saw the linen cloths lying there, but he did not go in. Then Simon Peter came, following him, and went into the tomb. He saw the linen cloths lying there, and the face cloth, which had been on

Jesus' head, not lying with the linen cloths but folded up in a place by itself. Then the other disciple, who had reached the tomb first, also went in, and he saw and believed; for as yet they did not understand the Scripture, that he must rise from the dead. Then the disciples went back to their homes" (John 20:1–10).

The Gospel ends with a further reference to Peter and John: "Peter turned and saw the disciple whom Jesus loved following them, the one who had been reclining at table close to him and had said, 'Lord, who is it that is going to betray you?' When Peter saw him, he said to Jesus, 'Lord, what about this man?' Jesus said to him, 'If it is my will that he remain until I come, what is that to you? You follow me!'" (John 21:20–22). Some then said that John was not going to die. But as John records, "Jesus did not say to him that he was not to die, but, 'If it is my will that he remain until I come, what is that to you?' This is the disciple who is bearing witness about these things, and who has written these things, and we know that his testimony is true" (verses 23–24). So the one "whom Jesus loved" is saying that his eyewitness account can be trusted.

Purpose for Writing

The Gospel of John was written at a time when Gnostic challenges to belief in the coming of Jesus as the Son of God had surfaced. We live in similar times, as authors, commentators, scholars and filmmakers question whether there is anything authentic about Christ or what is known as Christianity. Was Jesus a real person at all? Even if He was, according to this way of thinking, He certainly wasn't the Son of God. It is all an invention—a mere fabrication.

The Gospel of John is obviously quite different from the synoptic Gospels. It reads differently than Matthew, Mark and Luke. It is written with a different purpose. John wrote the Gospel from his perspective to demonstrate that Jesus is exactly who He said He was in the context of late-first-century doubt about Christ. And he included information about Jesus in the context of Hebrew life and law. He organized the work around the holy days and the festivals in Jewish life. Because part of the problem was that the Jewish leadership and many of the people had rejected Jesus as the Son of God, the Messiah to come, John set about to explain once more what happened in his experience.

Summarizing his purpose, he says, "Now Jesus did many other signs in the presence of the disciples, which are not written in this book; but these are written so that you may believe that Jesus is the Christ" (John 20:30–31).

If we accept that the Gospel of John was written before the three letters by his name, and before Revelation, then the content of the books makes sense. They can be understood sequentially.

For Jews but Also for Gentiles

As a Jew and an eyewitness, John had a lot to say about Judaism's rejection of the Christ. In the Gospel, there are 14 direct quotes from the Old Testament, or Hebrew Scriptures, supportive of Jesus as the Messiah. Half of them are from Psalms, four from Isaiah, two from Zechariah, and one from Exodus; in other words, from all three divisions of Scripture—the Law, the Prophets and the Writings (see also Luke 24:44). By the time John wrote at the end of the first century, false teachers had gone out into the world from all sides, and it was time to restate the truth about the identity of Jesus in terms that Judean Jews, Greek-speaking Jews, and gentiles could understand. Hence, the Gospel opens with a statement about the preeminence of Jesus as the preexisting expression of God—in Greek philosophical terms, the Logos, meaning "the Word."

We do not find direct references or quotes from the Old Testament in any of John's letters, however. That seems curious, because most New Testament writings contain some reference to the Hebrew Scriptures. But John had already laid out the scriptural evidence that Jesus is the Christ in his Gospel. Eventually people raised questions about the Gospel, and Gnostic false teaching began to contradict the truth about Jesus. So the first letter begins with a reminder in familiar terms of John's status as an eyewitness to Christ's coming (see John 1): "That which was from the beginning, which we have heard, which we have seen with our eyes, which we looked upon and have touched with our hands, concerning the word of life—the life was made manifest, and we have seen it, and testify to it and proclaim to you the eternal life, which was with the Father and was made manifest to us—that which we have seen and heard we proclaim also to you, so that you too may have fellowship with us; and indeed our fellowship is with the Father and with his Son Jesus Christ. And we are writing these things so that our joy may be complete" (1 John 1:1–4).

Gnostic Belief

John was combating the rising influence of Gnostic teachers who denied the testimony about Christ that had been given from the beginning of the Gospel. They claimed to have secret knowledge (gnosis). The opposition, they said, is between spirit (good) and matter (evil). They taught that the human sphere is corrupt and that God has nothing to do with it. Therefore Jesus could not have been the divine Christ but for a short time—from His baptism to just before his death. Nor could Christ have been killed; only the human Jesus was killed. Further, because God has nothing to do with this world, we can behave as we wish. Sin, in effect, doesn't matter.

So John writes, "This is the message we have heard from him and proclaim to you, that God is light, and in him is no darkness at all. If we say we have fellowship with him while we walk in darkness, we lie and do not practice the truth" (verses 5–6). It is easy to imagine the corrupting effect of the kind of teaching John was denouncing. He continues: "But if we walk in the light, as he is in the light, we have fellowship with one another, and the blood of Jesus his Son cleanses us from all sin. If we say we have no sin, we deceive ourselves, and the truth is not in us. If we confess our sins, he is faithful and just to forgive us our sins and to cleanse us from all unrighteousness. If we say we have not sinned, we make him a liar, and his word is not in us" (verses 7–10).

Sin is a reality. It exists. It cuts us off from God. It is not the way to live. But we do sin, and yet there is a way forward in God's sight. His Son's sacrificial death, John points out, has made a relationship with God possible and continues to do so, through the payment for sin and its forgiveness.

John's point is not to encourage sin by what he is saying, but simply to recognize that humans do sin even after conversion: "My little children, I am writing these things to you so that you may not sin. But if anyone does sin, we have an advocate with the Father, Jesus Christ the righteous. He is the propitiation [or atonement] for our sins, and not for ours only but also for the sins of the whole world" (1 John 2:1-2).

The Gnostics taught that they were above sin as followers of their version of Christ. They were more "spiritual" and did not need law to define behavior. But John continues with a reminder that obedience to God's way is evidence that we know Him. Anything else is a deceit: "And by this we know that we have come to know him, if we keep his commandments. Whoever says 'I know him' but does not keep his commandments is a liar, and the truth is not in him, but whoever keeps his word, in him truly the love of God is perfected. By this we may know that we are in him: whoever says he abides in him ought to walk in the same way in which he walked" (verses 3-6).

Next John says that the truth about Christ is what has been taught from the beginning. It is not a matter of discovering new esoteric knowledge such as the Gnostics claimed. Secret knowledge is not necessary, because God has revealed the truth about Christ from the start.

God and the Material World

John knows that God is concerned about the material world. That is the astounding thing about the Father and the Son. They have involved themselves with their creation to the extent of sacrificing sinless life for it, so that they can have an everlasting relationship with their children. The Gnostics, John notes, are walking in darkness, not light. This is evident because they have hatred for other humans: "Beloved, I am writing you no new commandment, but an old commandment that you had from the beginning. . . .

Whoever says he is in the light and hates his brother is still in darkness. Whoever loves his brother abides in the light, and in him there is no cause for stumbling. But whoever hates his brother is in the darkness and walks in the darkness, and does not know where he is going, because the darkness has blinded his eyes" (verses 7–11).

Now, you might wonder how this is relevant today. There are all kinds of variations on the theme that the Gnostics put forward. No doubt we have modern versions of the Gnosticism of John's time. We have those who deny that Christ ever existed, or who insist that the New Testament record is unreliable. We have New Age notions about what God is doing in the world. There is every kind of belief system, with people choosing what they want from all traditions. People claim a vague spirituality without much definition in terms of right behavior. They say, "I'm spiritual but not religious." It is as if people prefer anything but the truth delivered by God through Christ.

Despite God's involvement with the physical world, the first section of John's first letter ends with instruction about how to relate to it appropriately: "Do not love the world or the things in the world. If anyone loves the world, the love of the Father is not in him. For all that is in the world—the desires of the flesh and the desires of the eyes and pride in possessions—is not from the Father but is from the world. And the world is passing away along with its desires, but whoever does the will of God abides forever" (verses 15–17).

For the remainder of his first letter, John found it necessary to expose the error being introduced into the church by Gnostic teachers from without. He explained where truth, love and light really reside, and he discussed the disruption as showing that the end times had begun and that human society would have to be transformed.

Convinced that the end must be close because false teachers had multiplied and some of the believers were hearing their deceptive ideas, John issued a warning and a reminder of the truth: "Children, it is the last hour, and as you have heard that antichrist is coming, so now many antichrists have come. Therefore we know that it is the last hour" (1 John 2:18).

Confusion over teaching is a mark of the end times. Generally false teachers do not sound like deceivers. John is saying that the final supreme example of a false teacher known as Antichrist, or "anti-Christ," will yet come. But because that event is still in the future and falsehood is pandemic in the world's system, therefore antichrists (plural), precursors of the ultimate false teacher, will proliferate in the meantime. Sometimes they are even within the Church for a while: "They went out from us, but they were not of us; for if they had been of us, they would have continued with us. But they went out, that it might become plain that they all are not of us" (verse 19). Such people will come and go while the Church continues on.

What is the intention of an antichrist? It is surely to lead people away from Christ by deception. To offset any temptation to follow, John encourages his readers by reminding them of their calling and their acquired spiritual benefits. First, it is the Holy Spirit that has opened their minds to truth. He points out further that anyone who comes as a teacher and denies that Jesus is the Christ also denies the Father and is not on Their spiritual wavelength at all (verses 20–23).

It is important under such attacks to recall foundational teaching: "Let what you heard from the beginning abide in you. If what you heard from the beginning abides in you, then you too will abide in the Son and in the Father. And this is the promise that he made to us—eternal life." John goes on to say that the anointing of the Holy Spirit protects and informs the mind against falsehood. And so the believer is "to abide" in Christ, that is to say, to continue to live in Him, to remain with the Master (verses 24–27).

Continuing that relationship will result in confidence at Christ's return: "And now, little children, abide in him, so that when he appears we may have confidence and not shrink from him in shame at his coming. If you know that he is righteous, you may be sure that everyone who practices righteousness [or habitually lives the right way] has been born of him" (verses 28–29). The practice of right living, going the right way, separates the true follower from the Gnostic, who is a believer in falsehoods and who, as a result, habitually lives the wrong way.

Whose Children?

The truth is that God indeed specifically calls believers and imparts right knowledge. But this is also one of the reasons they go unrecognized in the world. A lack of acquaintance with God and His way means that those who don't follow Him cannot recognize those who do (1 John 3:1).

The future eternal form of God's people is as yet unknown. But as John points out, they will be like the resurrected returning Christ: "Beloved, we are God's children now, and what we will be has not yet appeared; but we know that when he appears we shall be like him, because we shall see him as he is." This knowledge should lead the believer to live a life of continuous spiritual improvement (verses 2–3).

John compares this with the activities of the one who is not dedicated to following God's way. That person is in effect a child of the adversary and habitually lives outside God's law of life. Sin is defined as living outside of law, and as John points out, Christ died so that sin can be forgiven: "Everyone who makes a practice of sinning also practices lawlessness; sin is lawlessness. You know that he appeared to take away sins, and in him there is no sin" (verses 4–5). The believer does not practice a wrong way of life. The choice is to be a child of God or a child of the arch-deceiver, the devil, whose works Christ came to annul: "No one who abides in him keeps on sinning. . . . Whoever makes a practice of sinning is of the devil, for the devil has been sinning from the beginning. The reason the Son of God appeared was to destroy the works of the devil. No one born of God makes a practice of sinning, for God's seed abides in him, and he cannot keep on sinning because he has been born of God" (verses 6–9).

Summarizing, John reminds his readers that the original way of right living taught by Christ included love of neighbor. He says, "By this it is evident who are the children of God, and who are the children of the devil: whoever does not practice righteousness is not of God, nor is the one who does not love his brother" (verse 10).

Brotherly Love

To explain more about brotherly love from God's perspective, John takes his audience all the way back to the beginning of human civilization: "For this is the message that you have heard from the beginning, that we should love one another. We should not be like Cain, who was of the evil one and murdered his brother. And why did he murder him? Because his own deeds were evil and his brother's righteous" (verses 11–12).

Envy of his brother's right living and guilt over his own failures caused Cain to murder his brother. It is always that way. Evil cannot bear righteousness. Therefore "do not be surprised, brothers, that the world hates you. . . . Everyone who hates his brother is a murderer, and you know that no murderer has eternal life abiding in him" (verses 13–15).

Christ's willingness to die for others should motivate us to sacrifice for the good of others. This defines godly love: "If anyone has the world's goods and sees his brother in need, yet closes his heart against him, how does God's love abide in him? Little children, let us not love in word or talk but in deed and in truth" (verses 17–18). John emphasizes that the practical meaning of loving rather than hating our brothers and sisters is that we provide for their needs. And as John's fellow apostle Paul pointed out years earlier, this reaching out includes all humanity—first the Church and then everyone else (Galatians 6:10).

Now John brings what he has said thus far to a conclusion. He notes that genuine love for believing brothers and sisters should give us confidence before God. We do not need to fear, because God is ready to forgive us and also to bless us for living according to his commandments and believing in Christ (1 John 3:19–24).

Expanding on Basic Teachings

John introduces the Spirit of God in preparation for what he is going to expand on next: how to distinguish God's Spirit from the spirit of antichrist, and what the Spirit of God produces in people.

"Beloved, do not believe every spirit, but test the spirits to see whether they are from God, for many false prophets have gone out into the world" (1 John 4:1). It is important in times of confusion over beliefs to know how to discern between truth and error. One way in respect of Christ, says John, is to determine whether a person accepts that He came from God and lived as a human being. If there is denial of Christ coming in the flesh, then "this is the spirit of the antichrist, which you heard was coming and now is in the world already" (verses 2–3).

John reinforces the fact that the Church knows the truth, and that the world knows its own, by saying, "Little children, you are from God and have overcome them, for he who is in you is greater than he who is in the world. They are from the world; therefore they speak from the world, and the world listens to them. We are from God. Whoever knows God listens to us; whoever is not from God does not listen to us. By this we know the Spirit of truth and the spirit of error" (verses 4–6).

John introduces the next section with the thought that because God loves His children, they should love each other. One of the reasons John has been called the apostle of love is that he writes so much about it. Yet he, along with his brother, was initially named by Christ a "son of thunder." We see evidence in his life of how God's Spirit at work in people molds and changes them over time, if they allow it to work. John became the apostle of love: "Beloved, let us love one another, for love is from God, and whoever loves has been born of God and knows God. Anyone who does not love does not know God, because God is love" (verses 7–8).

God's love for humanity was made plain by His willingness to send His only Son to pay the penalty for human sin by sacrificing His life in our place. If God can show love to that degree, should we not be able to love each other in this life (verses 9–11)?

John makes it clear that although no one has seen God, He is evident in the love that is being perfected in His people. This is a by-product of His Spirit at work. Further, John knew that his belief in Jesus Christ was based on his personal experience as an eyewitness: "And we have seen and testify that the Father has sent his Son to be the Savior of the world. Whoever confesses that Jesus is the Son of God, God abides in him, and he in God" (verses 12–15).

Returning to the theme of love and its connection with God and the blessing of a mind free of guilt and fear, John writes: "So we have come to know and to believe the love that God has for us. God is love, and whoever abides in love abides in God, and God abides in him. By this is love perfected with us, so that we may have confidence for the day of judgment, because as he is so also are we in this world" (verses 16–17). Jesus remains steadfast in the Father's love, and believers do too. This should give confidence as they live life in this world. There is no need for fear on this basis, because "perfect love casts out fear. For fear has to do with punishment, and whoever fears has not been perfected in love." John adds, "We love because he first loved us" (verses 18–19).

He continues by pointing out the hypocrisy of claiming to love God yet hating neighbor: "If anyone says, 'I love God,' and hates his brother, he is a liar; for he who does not love his brother whom he has seen cannot love God whom he has not seen. And this commandment we have from him: whoever loves God must also love his brother" (verses 20–21).

Defining the love of God, the apostle relates it to belief in Christ as God's Son, as well as to commandment keeping: "Everyone who believes that Jesus is the Christ has been born of God, and everyone who loves the Father loves whoever has been born of him. By this we know that we love the children of God, when we love God and obey his commandments. For this is the love of God, that we keep his commandments. And his commandments are not burdensome" (1 John 5:1–3). Though John is known as the apostle of love, he is not against law. In fact, he defines love in terms of commandment keeping.

Next he notes that the people of God are uniquely equipped to overcome the effects of living in this world cut off from God, because they have God's commands, God's Son and God's faith (verses 4–5).

Human, Yet Born of God

Returning to the theme that Christ came into the world and died as a human being and as the Son of God—as opposed to Gnostic teaching to the contrary—John says next: "This is he who came by water and blood—Jesus Christ; not by the water only but by the water and the blood. And the Spirit . . . testifies, because the Spirit is the truth" (verse 6).

It's important to say here that this is not a discussion about the Trinity. That discussion was not part of John's thinking or indeed of New Testament thinking. Notice the translation that follows: "For there are three that testify:

the Spirit and the water and the blood; and these three agree" (verses 7–8). That's to say that Jesus—as man yet also Son of God—is attested to by the Holy Spirit and thus there is agreement. This is spiritual knowledge, not human ideas. So John adds in the context of Gnostic teaching, "If we receive the testimony of men, the testimony of God is greater. . . . Whoever does not believe God has made him a liar, because he has not believed in the testimony that God has borne concerning his Son. And this is the testimony, that God gave us eternal life, and this life is in his Son. Whoever has the Son has life; whoever does not have the Son of God does not have life" (verses 9–12). Nonbelievers do not have the possibility of eternal life unless at some point they come to believe.

All of this tells us that it is God who has borne witness that Jesus is His Son who died, and that the Spirit of God convicts us of that if we are willing to listen to God, not men. Our eternal life depends on acceptance of Christ's submission to death on our behalf and of His resurrection by God.

In conclusion John says: "I write these things [the letter's contents] to you who believe in the name of the Son of God that you may know that you have eternal life" (verse 13). This summation of intent corresponds with John's comment in the Gospel: "But these are written so that you may believe that Jesus is the Christ, the Son of God, and that by believing you may have life in his name" (John 20:31).

Those who have a relationship with the Father will be able to ask for His help in many ways. The believer has the benefit of knowing that God hears prayers and will answer, including prayers for other brothers and sisters, who can repent of their sins and thus be forgiven: "If anyone sees his brother committing a sin not leading to death, he shall ask, and God will give him life—to those who commit sins that do not lead to death" (1 John 5:14–16a). This is not to say that God can forgive all sin, as John clarifies next. There are those who *will* not repent and therefore cannot have forgiveness extended to them. This is known as unpardonable sin: "There is sin that leads to death; I do not say that one should pray for that" (verse 16b). Defining sin, yet showing that forgiveness is possible for those who will repent and change, John adds: "All wrongdoing is sin, but there is sin that does not lead to death" (verse 17).

John concludes his first letter with three statements about what is important to know. The Gnostics claimed access to secret and superior knowledge. John has shown that their knowledge is inferior and erroneous. By contrast, "we know that everyone who has been born of God does not keep on sinning, but he who was born of God protects him, and the evil one does not touch him. We know that we are from God, and the whole world lies in the power of the evil one. And we know that the Son of God has come and has given us understanding, so that we may know him who is true; and we are in him who is true, in his Son Jesus Christ. He is the true God and eternal life" (verses 18–20).

Finally John adds, in what may seem a curious last thought, "Little children, keep yourselves from idols" (verse 21). Idols represent false gods, and idolatry is a sin that displaces the true God. Hence it is a summation of what the followers of Christ ("little children") must do throughout life.

Follow-Up Letters

The two remaining short letters deal with some of the same themes as the first letter but in more specific ways. Each is from "the elder," who is understood to be John. The second letter warns that false teachers are on their way to a specific congregation, and John advises what to do when they arrive. In the third letter he deals with a specific incident within the Church in the late first century. Both letters show the kind of behavior to which false teachers subjected the followers of Jesus.

John's emphasis on love among the brethren and for God's commandment continues. Personifying the Church as a woman, he says, "And now I ask you, dear lady—not as though I were writing you a new commandment, but the one we have had from the beginning—that we love one another. And this is love, that we walk according to his commandments; this is the commandment, just as you have heard from the beginning, so that you should walk in it" (2 John 5–6).

Gnostic antichrists are present all around and should not be welcomed among the people of God who "abide" in Christ: "For many deceivers have gone out into the world, those who do not confess the coming of Jesus Christ in the flesh. . . . Watch yourselves, so that you may not lose what we have worked for, but may win a full reward. . . . If anyone comes to you and does not bring this teaching, do not receive him into your house or give him any greeting, for whoever greets him takes part in his wicked works" (verses 7–11).

John concludes the second letter with the hope to come to see the brethren in person.

The third letter concerns a specific difficulty in one congregation founded through John's efforts. In John's absence a local leader took to lording it over people and became abusive of the believers and visitors. John writes to those who remain true to encourage right action and understanding of this man, who has gone so far as to banish people from the Church and to oppose John himself. John is clear about what will happen if he comes to them in person: "I will bring up what he is doing, talking wicked nonsense against us." The believers are encouraged to do what is right: "Beloved, do not imitate evil but imitate good. Whoever does good is from God; whoever does evil has not seen God" (verses 9–11).

John closes, as previously, with the hope to see them and not merely communicate with pen and ink.

The New Man

By the time we reach the end of these three letters, we see a very different John than the one named a "son of thunder" by Christ. His life in God's service brought spiritual growth and a depth that is evident. He became the last major apostolic defender of the faith and was about to receive the book of Revelation while exiled on the nearby island of Patmos for his beliefs. John would be used to deliver the apocalyptic vision that became the capstone to the New Testament.

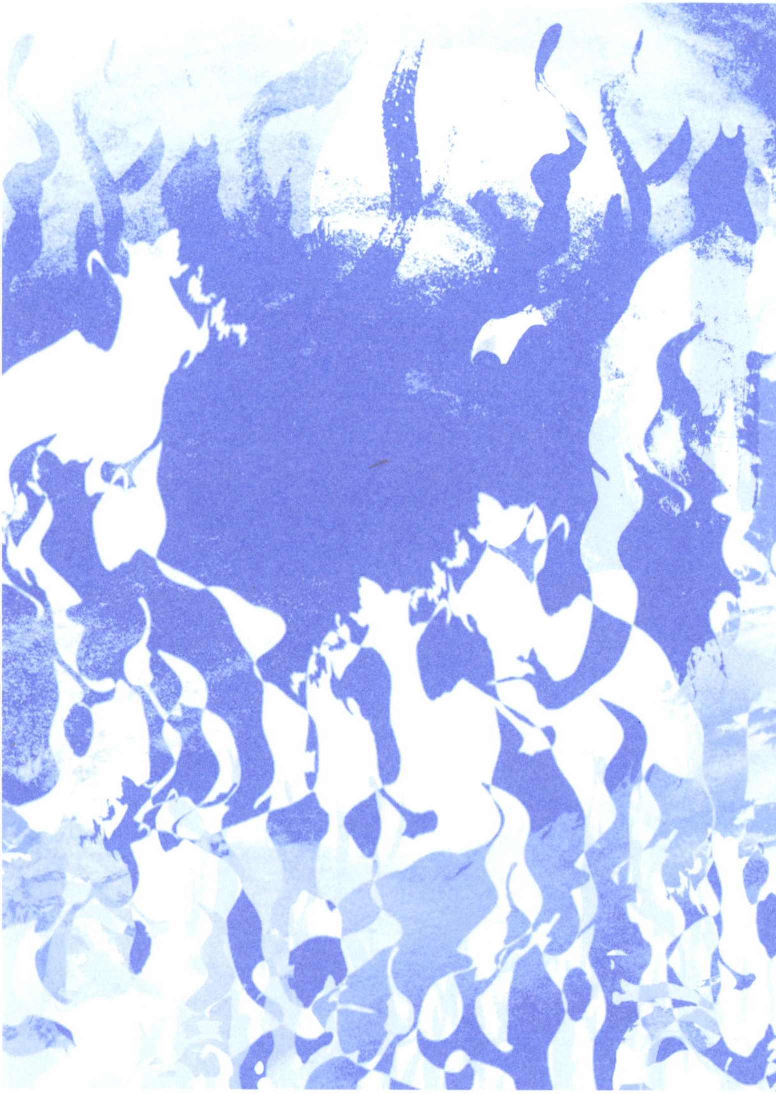

The End Times

"Immediately after the tribulation of those days the sun will be darkened, and the moon will not give its light, and the stars will fall from heaven, and the powers of the heavens will be shaken."

The apostle John's life was close to its end when he wrote down the content of the book of Revelation. It was around 95 C.E., and he was perhaps again in Ephesus following his exile on Patmos. His final written work concludes the collection we call the New Testament. It is also known as the Apocalypse, from the Greek term *apokalypsis*, meaning "the revealing" or "the unveiling" (in this case, of things to come). Because it is filled with strange visions, blood and smoke, terrifying warfare, fearsome beasts, and evil rulers, much of the book reads like a nightmare of the worst kind, though it eventually resolves in a new, peaceful world that is eternal. There are many who question the book's authorship. But conservative scholars, basing their opinion on the earliest traditions, believe Revelation to be an authentic work by the apostle John. Its themes extend John's Gospel and his three pastoral letters and provide the Church with an essential perspective on end-time events and the transformation of this Age of Man.

"The Unveiling" nevertheless remains obscure to most people who take the time to read it. Even notable theologians have stumbled over its contents. In the preface to early editions of Martin Luther's New Testament translation, the reformer famously said, "Let everyone think of it as his own spirit leads him." He judged the record of John's visions to be "neither apostolic nor prophetic," though over time he came to a different view. English Bible scholar J.B. Phillips expressed similar misgivings. He wrote in the introduction to his 20th-century version, "I was naturally tempted to omit this book altogether from my translational work." He noted that this was the course John Calvin had chosen in his New Testament commentary.

The spread of Gnostic ideas persuaded the apostle John that the last days had arrived. As already noted, tradition has it that toward the end of his life John was living at Ephesus. Growing opposition to the followers of Jesus likely brought about his exile on the nearby Roman island of Patmos. It was there that his final work was inspired. Later, perhaps back in Ephesus again, in obedience to the command to write down specific messages and the details of what he had seen in vision, he produced Revelation. As John records, looking back on his experience, "[I] was on the island called Patmos on account of the word of God and the testimony of Jesus [and heard a voice] saying, 'Write what you see in a book'" (Revelation 1:9b, 11a).

Author and Audience

The Apocalypse begins with a statement about the origin of its contents, its author and its purpose: "The revelation of Jesus Christ, which God gave him to show to his servants the things that must soon take place. He made it known by sending his angel to his servant John, who bore witness to the word of God and to the testimony of Jesus Christ, even to all that he saw" (Revelation 1:1–2).

God the Father gave Jesus the message about future events. Jesus in turn conveyed it to one of His followers, John, via an angel and through visions, so that God's people ("servants") would have foreknowledge of what was to happen at the end of this phase of human history. The early part of the text also contains important information for Jesus' followers with respect to how they should respond to their socio-political setting in light of what is to come. It is important to note that John did not claim the book as his personal work. As noted, he was commissioned to write down all he saw and heard—and send it in the form of an extended letter to seven church congregations (verses 4, 11, 19).

Private Knowledge

The book's opening verse clearly states that Revelation's initial audience was limited to the servants of God. John is "your brother and partner in the tribulation and the kingdom and the patient endurance that are in Jesus" (verse 9). This was not a public message at the time of its delivery. Today, of course, it is public in the sense that it appears in millions of Bibles in hundreds of languages and dialects. But that does not necessarily mean that this broader group has understood or will understand it. The book's reception throughout history proves otherwise. Despite its ready availability, most people have been puzzled by it.

The reason is bound up in a seldom-grasped biblical truth found in Matthew's Gospel. Jesus often spoke to the public using allegories. Matthew records a series of them that concern the kingdom of heaven. It is often thought that Jesus spoke this way to make his meaning clearer. But that is not what Matthew shows. Having heard Jesus publicly deliver the parable of the sower, His disciples asked Him, "'Why do you speak to them in parables?' And he answered them, 'To you it has been given to know the secrets of the kingdom of heaven, but to them it has not been given'" (Matthew 13:10–11).

The word *secrets* is translated from the Greek *musterion*, meaning "the unmanifested or private counsel of God, *(God's) secret*, the secret thoughts, plans, and dispensations of God . . . which are hidden from human reason, as well as from all other comprehension below the divine level, and await either fulfillment or revelation to those for whom they are intended" (W.F. Arndt, F.W. Danker, W. Bauer, *A Greek-English Lexicon of the New Testament and Other Early Christian Literature*, 2000).

Jesus said privately in explaining the parable of the sower to His followers, "This is why I speak to them in parables, because seeing they do not see, and hearing they do not hear, nor do they understand" (Matthew 13:13). The disciples were in a different category: "But blessed are your eyes, for they see, and your ears, for they hear" (verse 16).

John sheds further light on this private knowledge in his Gospel. He records the following response by Jesus to a disbelieving audience: "No one can come to me unless the Father who sent me draws him" (John 6:44). Shortly after this, as a result of Jesus' words, many who were initially open to Him "turned back and no longer walked with him" (verse 66). It comes as no surprise, then, to find that for the most part in the book of Revelation, the public has a very negative reaction to God and His message, and that the book is written for God's people as they await the Second Coming.

Thus John is writing *to the Church* when he says, "To him who loves us and has freed us from our sins by his blood and made us a kingdom, priests to his God and Father, to him be glory and dominion forever and ever. Amen. Behold, he is coming with the clouds, and every eye will see him, even those who pierced him, and all tribes of the earth will wail on account of him. Even so. Amen" (Revelation 1:5b–7). This is a message that would not make much sense to outsiders with its references to the Father; to Christ and His sacrifice, His return and His role; and to the future of His people.

Nor would the following have meaning for those outside the Church: "Worthy are you to take the scroll and to open its seals, for you were slain, and by your blood you ransomed people for God from every tribe and language and people and nation, and you have made them a kingdom and priests to our God, and they shall reign on the earth" (verses 9–10). John is writing *for the Church* when he records these words of angelic beings in praise of Christ.

Revelation's defined audience is indicated in many more passages throughout the book, including but not limited to chapter 6:9–11, regarding the martyrdom of believers; chapter 7:1–4, with its reference to the protection of God's people; chapter 8:1–4, which mentions the prayers of the saints; and chapter 12's identity and history of the Church.

The second and third chapters of the Apocalypse are especially Church-oriented in that they contain specific detailed messages to the seven congregations mentioned initially in chapter 1 (verse 11). Though the congregations are not named individually after the first three chapters, the book's postscript says, "I, Jesus, have sent my angel to testify to you about these things *for the churches*. I am the root and the descendant of David, the bright morning star" (Revelation 22:16, emphasis added). So Revelation begins and ends with a reference to its specific audience.

Seven Messages

The seven churches were located in the Roman province of Asia. They formed a loop beginning at Ephesus and proceeding north and east, then south and west, via Smyrna, Pergamum, Thyatira, Sardis, Philadelphia and Laodicea, and then back to Ephesus. But why were there only seven stops on John's itinerary? Were there only seven congregations in the region? It seems unlikely. We know that a few years earlier there were churches at Troas, northwest of Pergamum (Acts 20:5); at Miletus, south of Ephesus; and in the Lycus Valley at Colossae and Hierapolis, close to Laodicea (Colossians 1:2; 4:13).

It's helpful to note that the book of Revelation has many collections of seven—seven stars, seven angels, seven lampstands, seven seals, seven trumpets, seven heads, seven crowns, seven bowls and seven last plagues. In biblical literature, seven signifies completion, a totality, a whole. Thus the seven congregations represent the whole Church, and the messages to them have application to the whole Church throughout time to the present day and beyond. Each congregation received a message specific to it from Christ Himself (Revelation 1:11–20), to be read by all seven in the context of the entire book. John delivered these messages and records seven times throughout chapters 2 and 3, "He who has an ear, let him hear what the Spirit says to the churches" (see also 2:23).

Though the messages are individual, there are commonalities that lead to the conclusion that they deliver the same essential information repeated seven times for maximum impact. While the possibility of compromise of belief is evident in all locations, the more obvious common elements are commendation (except in the letter to Laodicea), rebuke (except in the letters to Smyrna and Philadelphia), exhortation, and an encouraging promise to those who will make the necessary personal changes.

Ephesus: Losing Zeal

Ephesus was a major port and the administrative center of Asia with a population of about 200,000. At the western end of a major highway, it housed one of seven wonders of the ancient world, the Temple of Artemis, or Diana. As such the city was named *neokoros* or "temple warden" of Artemis (see Acts 19:35). Ephesus also had a temple to Julius Caesar and the goddess Roma, and others to Augustus and later Hadrian. If cities wanted to attract funding and favor from Rome, they would ask permission to build such temples and would sometimes be granted the title *neokoros* as a result. Toward the end of the first century, the Ephesian city fathers proposed a shrine to the emperor Domitian (81–96 C.E.) and his dynasty. He agreed, and the Flavian family, which also included the emperors Vespasian and Titus (the destroyers of Jerusalem in 70 C.E.), was celebrated in a temple, the outlines of which can still be seen in the ruins of the city. As a result of Domitian's favor, Ephesus was named guardian of the emperor-worshiping imperial cult in Asia in about 89 C.E. Emperor worship involved offering sacrifices before the statues of the emperor(s).

It was probably during Domitian's reign that John was on the island of Patmos. The Greek writer Philostratus says that at the time the islands off the western coast were full of exiles. Was it that John refused to engage in emperor worship, having been reported by some opponents? Whatever the cause of his stay on Patmos, it did not last long. Domitian's successor, Nerva (96–98 C.E.), freed all exiles not guilty of serious infractions. If John now returned to Ephesus, he was free there to write down and distribute the account of what he had seen and heard.

Christ's message to the Ephesian church begins, "I know your works, your toil and your patient endurance, and how you cannot bear with those who are evil, but have tested those who call themselves apostles and are not, and found them to be false. I know you are enduring patiently and bearing up for my name's sake, and you have not grown weary" (Revelation 2:2–3).

In its early years, the church at Ephesus was characterized by zeal, by patience in trying circumstances, and by a devotion to good works. They were even willing to question the authority of people claiming to be apostles but who came with a false message. Being a crossroads city, Ephesus attracted certain kinds of people, including wandering religious teachers.

An example of this from Paul's time in Ephesus is found in the book of Acts. Luke writes, "Then some of the itinerant Jewish exorcists undertook to invoke the name of the Lord Jesus over those who had evil spirits, saying, "I adjure you by the Jesus whom Paul proclaims" (Acts 19:13). The later false teachers who said they were apostles fit into this category of itinerant teachers. The church at Ephesus had been faithful in many ways and had not compromised by listening to such people. But in other ways they had let down. They had become neglectful, and their good works were no excuse for not changing where they needed to. So John's letter also had some words of warning from Christ: "I have this against you, that you have abandoned the love you had at first. Remember therefore from where you have fallen; repent, and do the works you did at first. If not, I will come to you and remove your lampstand from its place, unless you repent" (Revelation 2:4–5).

The low character of surrounding society had affected the church. It had grown less enthusiastic about the truth that Paul had first taught. Now 30 to 40 years later, the fervor that the church at first felt for its new knowledge had lessened. This can happen to anyone. This is why the message to the Ephesian church was to wake up, to recognize their sad state, and to repent, or change. Christ told them to remember the excitement of their first commitment to His way of life. He knew that they were capable of holding firm. He indicates this in His next statement: "Yet this you have: you hate the works of the Nicolaitans, which I also hate" (verse 6). Apparently the Ephesians were still able to distinguish between right and wrong in respect of this group—followers of a man named Nicolas, who taught that it was possible to be a believer and still commit immoral acts. This would have been a convenient argument for those who wanted to compromise.

The Ephesian congregation, then, had grown less zealous, but they had not succumbed completely to the pressure to compromise their high moral ideals. Christ's message to the Ephesians ends with a warning and a promise to His followers in all times: "He who has an ear, let him hear what the Spirit says to the churches. To the one who conquers I will grant to eat of the tree of life, which is in the paradise of God" (verse 7).

Smyrna: Hold Fast

Smyrna, about 40 miles or 65 kilometers north of Ephesus, had a population of about 100,000. The city was known for its wealth, beautiful buildings, good wines, science and medicine. In 195 B.C.E., Smyrna had become the first city in Asia to build a shrine to the goddess Roma. It was also a port city and vied with Ephesus and nearby Pergamum for imperial favor by setting up temples to the emperors. In 23 C.E. it was granted permission to build a temple honoring Tiberius, his mother (Livia) and the Senate. That temple led to Tiberius bestowing on the city the coveted title *neokoros*—temple warden of his imperial cult.

It seems that by John's time the Jews at Smyrna had begun to oppose the followers of the Way. He records the opening of Christ's message: "The words of the first and the last, who died and came to life. 'I know your tribulation and your poverty (but you are rich) and the slander of those who say that they are Jews and are not, but are a synagogue of Satan'" (verses 8–9). The confrontation between Christ's followers and the Jews had come to a head, and perhaps the Jews were turning them in to the authorities, charging them with anti-Roman behavior. There is certainly evidence that such denunciations and resulting punishments took place during the rule of Emperor Trajan (98–117) in the nearby province of Pontus-Bithynia, according to a letter from Pliny the Younger to the emperor written between 110 and 113.

Jesus' message to the church at Smyrna was one of encouragement to hold fast: "Do not fear what you are about to suffer. Behold, the devil is about to throw some of you into prison, that you may be tested, and for ten days you will have tribulation. Be faithful unto death, and I will give you the crown of life" (verse 10). This was a time of intense persecution. And some would even have to die for their beliefs. The followers in Smyrna needed a message to fortify those who would pay the ultimate price of faith.

The willingness to do what is inconvenient or unpopular, even in the face of suffering, is vitally important in all ages. The second message concludes with the encouragement to go forward despite the obstacles, because the reward is unparalleled—eternal life: "He who has an ear, let him hear what the Spirit says to the churches. The one who conquers will not be hurt by the second death" (verse 11). The "second death" is a reference to the fate of those who will knowingly refuse to go God's way once their eyes are opened.

The potential for compromise reflected in the case of Smyrna concerns putting submission to humans ahead of loyalty to God.

Pergamum: "Satan's Throne"

Pergamum (Pergamos or Pergamon) has a history stretching back to at least the fourth or fifth century B.C.E. In 133 B.C.E., the last remaining ruler of the Pergamene dynasty, Attalus III, willed the city to Rome. Known for its high level of culture, Pergamum fostered early aspects of what we know today as the medical arts and psychotherapy. With health-giving springs and a medical center named after the Roman god Asklepius, the city attracted people from all over the known world.

In John's time, Pergamum was one of the largest cities in the province of Asia, with a population of about 120,000 people. It was also the location of various pagan shrines. Its temple for Athena was attached to a library of 200,000 volumes that rivaled the great Egyptian library at Alexandria. The use of parchment made from animal skins and bound into books was perfected in Pergamum, the word *parchment* coming from the name of the city. The city's elaborate centerpiece was the altar to Zeus, celebrating the Pergamene victory over the Gauls in 190 B.C.E. Much of the altar was removed in the late 19th century and can be seen in Berlin's Pergamon Museum. Priests are said to have offered sacrifices at the altar 24 hours a day, seven days a week. The dominance of this pagan structure, set on a volcanic plug high above the surrounding countryside, may explain the reference to "Satan's throne" in the message to the believers there (verse 13). The association of altars with thrones is an ancient one. It may be that "Satan's throne" also refers to the cult of Asklepius, symbolized by a serpent (Revelation 12:9 names Satan as "that ancient serpent"). Another possibility is the fact that Pergamum was the seat of Rome's power to persecute those in the region who would not participate in the imperial cult. It was, after all, the first city in Asia to build a temple to an emperor (Augustus), and it became the center for the imperial cult generally in the province. Soon after John recorded Revelation, the area adjacent to the altar saw the construction of a new temple to the emperor Trajan (98–117).

Through John, Christ identifies Himself as the One "who has the sharp two-edged sword"—that is to say, the encouraging and corrective Word of God that comes from His mouth. He continues, "I know where you dwell, where Satan's throne is. Yet you hold fast my name, and you did not deny my faith even in the days of Antipas my faithful witness, who was killed among you, where Satan dwells" (verses 12–13).

Antipas is thought to have been the first follower of Christ to be martyred in Pergamum. Later tradition says that during the emperor Domitian's reign, he suffered a gruesome fate, being slowly roasted to death in a brass kettle.

Not all that happened in the congregation in Pergamum brought commendation. Christ's message also included a complaint: "But I have a few things against you: you have some there who hold the teaching of Balaam, who taught Balak to put a stumbling block before the sons of Israel, so that they might eat food sacrificed to idols and practice sexual immorality. So also you have some who hold the teaching of the Nicolaitans. Therefore repent. If not, I will come to you soon and war against them with the sword of my mouth" (verses 14–16).

The reference to Balaam is to the event where a pagan priest cunningly counseled the Moabites on how to get the Old Testament Israelites to sin (Numbers 22:3–6; 31:16). He did so by blending sexual immorality and idol worship. This explains the second reference in the book to the Nicolaitans. As at Ephesus, the followers of Nicolas were active in Pergamum at the time of John, and the pressure to conform to false teaching with respect to immorality must have been very strong. The message to the church there is rounded out with a statement for every follower of Christ caught in compromise over sexual immorality: "He who has an ear, let him hear what the Spirit says to the churches. To the one who conquers I will give some of the hidden manna, and I will give him a white stone, with a new name written on the stone that no one knows except the one who receives it" (verse 17). Believers who will not compromise—and so overcome or conquer—will be given eternal life, symbolized here by access to God's spiritual food in contrast to "food sacrificed to idols," and favorable judgment (the white stone), and a new name that will identify them as God's own immortal children.

Thyatira: Tolerating Immorality

The message from Jesus Christ to Thyatira was again specific to the problems the city posed for His followers. According to legend, Thyatira, about 35 miles or 55–60 kilometers inland from Pergamum, was first established as a center for the worship of the sun god, Apollo Tyrimnaeus. It passed through Macedonian, Seleucid and Pergamene possession until Pergamum and its possessions were gifted to Rome in 133 B.C.E.

Today all that can be seen of the ancient city are a few scattered ruins in the center of modern-day Akhisar. But from inscriptions discovered, it was a wealthy city with many trade guilds under the patronage of various pagan deities. The guilds were therefore much more religious in practice than might be assumed. Their feasts were held in local pagan temples. According to the *Word Biblical Commentary*, the associations' members were "clothiers, bakers, tanners, potters, linen workers, wool merchants, slave traders, shoemakers, dyers, and copper smiths."

The dyers guild was especially successful. A follower of Jesus who came from Thyatira was a woman named Lydia. She was a seller of purple dye or purple cloth, and was associated with Paul's ministry in Philippi (Acts 16:14–15, 40).

Bronze workers formed another guild. This may explain partly a reference in the letter. To the angel of the church in Thyatira, John was to write: "The words of the Son of God, who has eyes like a flame of fire, and whose feet are like burnished bronze" (Revelation 2:18). Christ is referred to here as "the Son of God"—the only place this title occurs in Revelation. It is therefore significant and may be stated for emphasis to a city that engaged heavily in the imperial cult and viewed the emperor as a son of god and also as the sun god in the flesh. This Son of God shone more brightly than the local sun god and guild patron.

Despite the difficult circumstances surrounding the church in Thyatira, they earned Christ's commendation for "your works, your love and faith and service and patient endurance, and that your latter works exceed the first" (verse 19). However, like other churches in the province of Asia, they were corrected for certain problems: "But I have this against you, that you tolerate that woman Jezebel, who calls herself a prophetess and is teaching and seducing my servants to practice sexual immorality and to eat food sacrificed to idols" (verse 20). The Thyatiran church had been seduced into following some of the practices of the pagan society around them, specifically listening to Gnostic false teaching and giving themselves sexual license—becoming permissive. It seems that they were plagued by a particular kind of seduction involving temple sex and food offered to idols. Literally or figuratively, this deception was related to one named Jezebel, perhaps a guild leader and no doubt viewed as a counterpart of the infamous idolatrous queen of ancient Israel (1 Kings 18–21; 2 Kings 9).

The message to the Thyatiran church is clear, and it demonstrates that sometimes Christ speaks very plainly: "I gave [Jezebel] time to repent, but she refuses to repent of her sexual immorality. Behold, I will throw her onto a sickbed, and those who commit adultery with her I will throw into great tribulation, unless they repent of her works, and I will strike her children dead. And all the churches will know that I am he who searches mind and heart, and I will give to each of you according to your works" (Revelation 2:21–23). This is a very powerful passage. Jesus Christ is concerned about hearts and minds, about private and public standards. But He is always fair, just and merciful. He simply wants to see repentance and behavioral change.

There were some in Thyatira who did not fall under His judgment. They had not compromised, and the statement to them highlights another potential problem: "But to the rest of you in Thyatira, who do not hold this teaching, who have not learned what some call the deep things of Satan, to you I say, I do not lay on you any other burden. Only hold fast what you have until I come" (verses 24–25). The phrase "the deep things of Satan" is probably a reference to the Gnostic idea that in order for a person to overcome Satan, he or she had to experience evil deeply. The Gnostics believed that since the body was made of matter and was therefore evil, breaking spiritual laws was of no consequence. This led to much licentiousness and an "anything goes" mentality—much like we see in society today.

The message to the Thyatiran church closes with a familiar promise of purposeful eternal life: "The one who conquers and who keeps my works until the end, to him I will give authority over the nations, and he will rule them with a rod of iron, as when earthen pots are broken in pieces, even as I myself have received authority from my Father. And I will give him the morning star. He who has an ear, let him hear what the Spirit says to the churches" (verses 26–29).

The form of compromise here was permissiveness in personal life, attempting to mingle society's ways with the worship of God.

Sardis: As Good as Dead

Sardis, about 40 miles or 65 kilometers southeast of Thyatira, was an ancient city of wealth and commerce, the capital of the Lydian kingdom and home to the legendary King Croesus. Its wealth came from the gold found in its River Pactolus and from its textiles. The world's first coinage, made from a gold-silver alloy, was introduced at Sardis. At the intersection of various trade routes, it was also the end of the 5th-century-B.C.E. Royal Road from Susa. The Persians, the Greeks, the Seleucids, the Pergamenes and the Romans ruled Sardis in succession. Parts of the Ionic temple to Artemis of Seleucid times can still be seen, as well as what remains of the acropolis of Croesus. After an earthquake destroyed much of the city in 17 C.E., it was rebuilt with help from the emperors Tiberius and Claudius.

With an estimated population of 60–100,000, Sardis was home to a large Jewish community in the time of the early Church. It is mentioned in the Hebrew Scriptures as "Sepharad" (see Obadiah 20) and may have become a place for Jewish émigrés in the centuries following the fall of Jerusalem in 586 B.C.E. The first-century Jewish historian Josephus tells us that there were sufficient wealthy Jews there in his time to send temple tax to Jerusalem. Therefore it would have been a natural place for the apostles' teaching to take root. As we have noted earlier, it was Paul's custom to try to address those in the synagogues first, since they were literate in the Scriptures.

Christ's message to the church in Sardis begins: "The words of him who has the seven spirits of God and the seven stars. I know your works. You have the reputation of being alive, but you are dead" (Revelation 3:1). Here was a group of believers who were thought to be alive and vigorous, and yet by God's standards they were as good as dead. Again, the lesson is clear: Christ's followers are supposed to exhibit their faith by doing, by consistently living a way of life. There has to be more than just a show of righteousness. True followers have to demonstrate their belief by action, both toward God and toward their fellow human beings.

The message to the church here is again very strong: "Wake up, and strengthen what remains and is about to die, for I have not found your works complete in the sight of my God. Remember, then, what you received and heard. Keep it, and repent. If you will not wake up, I will come like a thief, and you will not know at what hour I will come against you" (verses 2–3).

There were, of course, some, as in any congregation, who were faithful to their belief. And Christ did not forget them. The One whose eyes were like a flame of fire could recognize His faithful servants: "Yet you have still a few names in Sardis, people who have not soiled their garments, and they will walk with me in white, for they are worthy" (verse 4).

And then follows the promise of eternal life for the active and committed follower of Christ: "The one who conquers will be clothed thus in white garments, and I will never blot his name out of the book of life. I will confess his name before my Father and before his angels. He who has an ear, let him hear what the Spirit says to the churches" (verses 5–6).

Once again, this plain and direct letter contains strong correction. The Church members in Sardis were to overcome spiritual lethargy—their form of compromise. But there was also encouragement for the congregation. Christ reminded them of the incredible future that lay ahead of them. But they had to play their part.

Philadelphia: Faithfully Committed

Philadelphia, some 28 miles (45 kilometers) southeast of Sardis, was commercially significant as a wine-producing community located at the foot of Asia's central high plateau. The city's name means "brotherly love," possibly so called because Attalus II of Pergamum, whose fraternal loyalty earned him the epithet "Philadelphus," dedicated the city to his brother King Eumenes in the mid-second century B.C.E. Another claim is that the Egyptian Ptolemy Philadelphus founded the city after he took possession of territories in Asia Minor in the previous century. What is known for sure is that the Romans granted the city relief from taxation and gave aid when it suffered the devastating earthquake of 17 C.E. In gratitude, the local leaders added "Neocaesarea" to the city's name. Later, in John's time, it became Philadelphia Flavia in honor of the emperor Vespasian (69–79) of the Flavian line.

To the church in Philadelphia, Christ instructed John to write: "The words of the holy one, the true one, who has the key of David, who opens and no one will shut, who shuts and no one opens. I know your works. Behold, I have set before you an open door, which no one is able to shut. I know that you have but little power, and yet you have kept my word and have not denied my name" (verses 7–8).

This is signifying that when Jesus Christ makes a decision, it has power, it has finality, and no man can interfere with that decision. The congregation lacked the outward appearance of spiritual power. Yet they were humble, and they had a faithful commitment to Christ's way of life. But they, too, faced problems. It seems that in this city there was a group of Jews who claimed to be religious and were not. They persecuted the followers of Christ: "Behold, I will make those of the synagogue of Satan who say that they are Jews and are not, but lie—behold, I will make them come and bow down before your feet and they will learn that I have loved you. Because you have kept my word about patient endurance, I will keep you from the hour of trial that is coming on the whole world, to try those who dwell on the earth" (verses 9–10).

The Philadelphians would ultimately triumph over their persecutors. This is a promise with applications to believers in all ages. It assures us of God's involvement in our security, physical or spiritual, no matter the circumstances. Here we are told that the faithful will be kept from a time of great difficulty. The true follower who is faithful and is overcoming personal problems in life will have divine help in times of trouble. A committed believer lives each day as if it could be the last. This is one meaning of the concluding thoughts to Philadelphians: they will ultimately gain eternal life. "I am coming soon," says Christ. "Hold fast what you have, so that no one may seize your crown. The one who conquers, I will make him a pillar in the temple of my God. Never shall he go out of it, and I will write on him the name of my God, and the name of the city of my God, the new Jerusalem, which comes down from my God out of heaven, and my own new name. He who has an ear, let him hear what the Spirit says to the churches" (verses 11–13).

The followers of Christ at Philadelphia pleased God with their patience, their humility and their willingness to obey. Therefore they were promised an even closer relationship with God in His new world. They were encouraged not to compromise in the face of religious persecution.

Laodicea: Neither Hot nor Cold

Laodicea, about 40 miles (65 kilometers) southeast of Philadelphia and 100 miles (160 kilometers) east of Ephesus, was well known for the production of beautiful black wool, for banking and for the practice of medical arts. Because of the region's volcanic and seismic activity, at nearby Hierapolis there was a Roman spa resort with hot thermal baths. Neighboring Colossae had cold water springs. About 30 years earlier, the apostle Paul had ministered to congregations in all three locations. By the time of John's writing of Revelation, Laodicea was the church for which the greatest correction was reserved. It seems that Laodicea's water supply was lukewarm. The seven letters come to a climax with a terrible warning for the compromising Christian who is spiritually neither hot nor cold.

To the church in Laodicea, John was to write: "The words of the Amen, the faithful and true witness, the beginning of God's creation. I know your works: you are neither cold nor hot. Would that you were either cold or hot! So, because you are lukewarm, and neither hot nor cold, I will spit you out of my mouth" (verses 14–16). Lukewarmness is a symbol for the compromise that comes with spiritual pride, or self-sufficiency. And that is plainly not a characteristic that Jesus Christ wants to see in His followers.

Laodicea was also a prosperous city—in part because it was at the junction of ancient trade routes. But wealth caused problems for Laodicea: "For you say, I am rich, I have prospered, and I need nothing, not realizing that you are wretched, pitiable, poor, blind, and naked" (verse 17). Laodicea's self-sufficiency masked an underlying spiritual poverty. But there was an antidote: "I counsel you to buy from me gold refined by fire, so that you may be rich, and white garments so that you may clothe yourself and the shame of your nakedness may not be seen, and salve to anoint your eyes, so that you may see" (verse 18).

The commodities spoken of here would have been well known to any Laodicean. Gold was a familiar item. But spiritual treasure—an uncompromising commitment to Christ, tested under difficult circumstances—would have been hard to find among the lax followers in Laodicea. Christ's recommendation that the Laodiceans put on white clothes (the symbol of righteousness)—as opposed to their famous black woolen cloth—was a reminder of their spiritual nakedness.

Finally, Christ prescribed an ointment cure for the eyes, so that the Laodiceans could see spiritually. It is thought that the city made an eye salve, but the Laodicean church needed its spiritual vision healed more than it needed a physical remedy. Christ expresses His love and concern with these words: "Those whom I love, I reprove and discipline, so be zealous and repent. Behold, I stand at the door and knock. If anyone hears my voice and opens the door, I will come in to him and eat with him, and he with me" (verses 19–20).

The message is clear: spiritual self-sufficiency needs correction. The faithful are going to respond to such advice and change, and Jesus Christ is always willing to help. The letter to the Laodicean church ends with a remarkable invitation and the promise of limitless life: "The one who conquers, I will grant him to sit with me on my throne, as I also conquered and sat down with my Father on his throne" (verse 21).

Seven Messages, One Point

What John set down in the first section of Revelation is the preface for all that follows. The messages to the seven churches—and to the Church through time—are about resisting various pressures to compromise in a world that is not God's and will not be His until all that is described in the expansive remainder of the book comes about. Compromise can be the result of personal negligence (Ephesus), putting allegiance to humans ahead of loyalty to God (Smyrna), sexual immorality and idolatry (Pergamum), permissiveness (Thyatira), spiritual lethargy (Sardis), religious persecution (Philadelphia), or self-sufficiency (Laodicea). Each of the seven messages contains urgent information for Christ's followers then and in all ages: stand firm in the face of society's pressure to conform; do not compromise basic beliefs or forsake Christ's example.

These are timeless human conditions. Followers need God's help to avoid compromise in any of these categories. The overall message is obvious: whatever the form of the compromise, it is wrong and unacceptable to Jesus Christ and will not enable the follower to stand when difficult times come.

John's account of what he saw and was told to write now moves to the panorama of human history that must unfold as the present age comes to its climax. Though we cannot know exactly when this era of human self-government will end, nor the precise moment of Jesus Christ's return, the Apocalypse does unveil the kind of world that will precede

His coming. It also teaches those who have ears to hear, how they must distance themselves from the way of man—typified by the "government of Caesar"—and anticipate, by their way of living, the coming sovereignty of God and His Son.

The Context of Revelation

After Jesus' departure, the community of His followers continued in the beliefs and practices of the God of Abraham, Isaac and Jacob, empowered by the Holy Spirit with new understanding. They knew that the Hebrew Scriptures were a unified whole. Thus, when the seven churches and subsequently the broader Church read John's writings, they connected many things he said with that body of Scripture and also with the more recent oral and written teaching they had received. For them the Hebrew Scriptures and the apostolic writings that followed represented unified practice and belief.

The only way for the called-out ones to understand Revelation was by the mediation of the Holy Spirit and by contextualizing the lengthy letter in light of the rest of Scripture. When the Bible is read holistically, Revelation is consistent with its other parts. This means that, in particular, Ezekiel, Daniel, Zechariah, Jesus, Matthew, Mark, Luke, John, Paul, James, Peter and Jude all make a significant contribution to the content of Revelation.

For example, the description of God's throne (Revelation 4) recalls Ezekiel's similar vision (Ezekiel 1). In the later chapters of his prophecy, Ezekiel writes about the establishment of the kingdom of God on earth. This finds parallels in the final chapters of Revelation.

The well-known Four Horsemen of the Apocalypse (Revelation 6) are reminiscent of the prophet Zechariah's description of four similar horses (Zechariah 1 and 6) and of Jesus' private reply to His disciples about the end of the age in Matthew 24. There He also made reference to the book of Daniel and to specific coming events in the Middle East (Matthew 24:15). Further, He mentioned His own return in the kind of language found in Revelation 19.

Daniel's visions, in which various empires that have ruled the Middle East are represented by a statue of a man and by several animals (see Daniel 2, 7 and 8), are paralleled by John's vision of composite beasts in Revelation 13 and 17.

The apostle Paul wrote about Christ's second coming in each of his letters, also to a set of seven local or regional churches—in Thessalonica, Corinth, Galatia, Rome, Colossae, Ephesus and Philippi. Similarly, in personal letters to the small groups of believers in their care, James, Peter and Jude all wrote about the great future event that would eclipse the "present age." It is in the nature of such messages that they are intended principally for a small part of the whole. For the seven congregations in Asia Minor at the close of the first century, the Scriptures were all background to Revelation's record of end-time events.

It is clear that so many parts of the Bible are interconnected and consistent with each other. When we connect the dots, it becomes obvious that one day God will intervene to resolve human problems. Through John, the followers of Jesus Christ have been given insights into God's plan for bringing the kingdom of man to a close and establishing the kingdom of God. What they cannot know ahead of time is precisely how every prophecy will be fulfilled. They can know the outlines of how society will develop until God must intervene. They cannot know the timing of Christ's return, as Christ Himself does not (Matthew 24:36). But they can be prepared for that day by personal vigilance about their spiritual state and by thus being ready (Matthew 24:44).

God's Throne

Following the messages to the seven congregations, John is taken in vision via an open door to God's throne. The privileged access will allow him to be shown "what must take place after this" (Revelation 4:1). This section of John's account continues through chapter 6:17 and is the longest of six throne-room scenes (the others are found in 7:9–17; 11:15–19; 14:1–5; 15:2–8; and 19:1–8). It provides the introduction to all the remaining visions of the book.

In chapter 4, John sees the Father's heavenly throne with the backdrop of a rainbow that resembles an emerald, resting on a sea of crystal, surrounded by four angelic creatures with the face of a lion, an ox, a man and an eagle. Further, there are 24 more angelic beings, termed "elders," who worship Him along with the four creatures at the throne. Much of this description of God's throne is a variation of the visions in Ezekiel 1:4–28 and Isaiah 6, while the heavenly council is indicated in 1 Kings 22 and Job 1 and 2, among other references. John describes the elders as worshiping God and saying, "Worthy are you, our Lord and God, to receive glory and honor and power" (Revelation 4:11). This is a counter to the adulation offered to the Roman emperors who were also addressed as "our Lord and our God." But the God of John's vision is the one who "created all things, and by [His] will they existed and were created"—something the emperors could not claim.

Chapter 5 introduces what John saw and heard next: the Lamb of God (Christ) as the only One who is worthy to break the seven seals of a mysterious scroll in God's hand, to the praise of all the heavenly beings. This leads to the immediate breaking of six of the seals (Revelation 6:1–17), followed by an interlude (chapter 7) and then the breaking of the seventh seal (Revelation 8:1). Each seal represents a condition or event in God's eschatological plan. Again, the reason that John is delivering the information is that it is "the revelation of Jesus Christ, which God gave him to show to his servants the things that must soon take place" (Revelation 1:1).

The Seven Seals

At the breaking of the first four seals by Christ, four horses and their riders (Revelation 6:2–8) are set free to roam the earth. The first is a white horse, its rider carrying a bow and wearing a crown. The rider "[comes] out conquering, and to conquer." He would be recognizable to John's audience as an Apollo-like sun-god figure and stand for politico-religious deception, the archetypical false messiah. Next comes a bright red horse with a rider who carries a great sword, signifying widespread war. He takes "peace from the earth," causing people to kill each other. The third is a black horse; its rider carries a pair of scales, and a heavenly voice indicates that scarcity and famine follow. The fourth horse is pale (gray or yellowish green) and represents pestilence and disease. Death is its rider, accompanied by the Grave. The apocalyptic sections of the synoptic Gospels provide helpful background in understanding these horses and their riders. Jesus explained that several long-term conditions would precede His return. They include messianic deception, war, famine and pestilence; see, for example, Matthew 24:3-8; Mark 13:5-8; and Luke 21:8-11.

When the fifth seal is broken, the martyrs of God through the ages cry out to be avenged, asking how much longer they must wait. They are told that a little more time must pass until others yet to be persecuted will meet their end (Revelation 6:9-11). The fifth seal, then, corresponds to the persecution of Christ's followers mentioned in Matthew 24:9-10.

A great earthquake accompanies the opening of the sixth seal (Revelation 6:12-14). There are disturbances in the heavens—the moon turns red like blood, the sun becomes black, the stars fall from the sky, which is rolled up like a scroll. This parallels Jesus' words in Matthew's Gospel: "Immediately after the tribulation of those days the sun will be darkened, and the moon will not give its light, and the stars will fall from heaven, and the powers of the heavens will be shaken" (Matthew 24:29).

Before describing the events associated with the breaking of the seventh seal, John tells of two select groups of people (Revelation 7:1-8, 9-17). The first is the 144,000 who are protected by God (with a different kind of seal) from the worst aspects of God's intervention. This is reminiscent of a passage in the book of Ezekiel, where an angel puts a mark of protection on the forehead of those who are concerned with sin in the city of Jerusalem (Ezekiel 9:4-6). The 144,000 are listed in groups of 12,000 from 12 of the tribes of Israel. The entire group has been explained as 12 tribes x 12 apostles x 1,000—a symbol for the elect of God, the followers of Christ across time. In Revelation 14:1–5, they appear with Christ on Mount Zion. It is said that they "follow the Lamb wherever he goes. These have been redeemed from mankind as firstfruits for God and the Lamb" (verse 4). Once again we see that John is writing for the benefit of the Church, encouraging them with a view of their future.

The second group mentioned in this interlude chapter is much larger and is present during the end time "great tribulation" (see Matthew 24:21). This is the means by which they come into an eternal relationship with God.

John's description of the seventh seal comprises initially chapters 8:1 through 11:19. This length is necessary to describe the sevenfold nature of the seventh seal. Divided into seven separate events heralded by angelic trumpet blasts, the opening of this seal starts the countdown to Christ's return.

The Seven Trumpets

Seven angels who attend God's throne are each given a trumpet. The first four trumpets precipitate plagues that fall on the earth. First come hail, fire and blood that devastate one third of the earth's trees and grass. Next is a plague in what appears to be a burning mountain thrown into the sea and affecting a third of the sea, its creatures and the ships that sail it. When the third angel sounds, a flaming poisonous star falls to the earth affecting a third of rivers and springs. Many people die as a result. The fourth plague strikes the sun, moon and stars, obliterating a third of their light. An eagle flies overhead, warning of the three trumpet blasts to come and crying "Woe, woe, woe to those who dwell on earth" (Revelation 8:6–13).

The fifth angel's blast (Revelation 9:1–11) causes a star to fall from heaven and open the Abyss or "bottomless pit," releasing demonic powers on the earth to torment for five months, but not kill, those who have not been sealed. The demons' leader is named Abaddon and Apollyon ("destruction" and "the one who destroys"). He is Satan the Devil.

Further devastation awaits with the sixth trumpet plague. Four angels who have been bound at the River Euphrates are released, possibly a symbol of four nations in that region. With a cavalry of 200 million, their task is to destroy one third of mankind. Despite the destruction, "the rest of mankind, who were not killed by these plagues, did not repent of the works of their hands nor give up worshiping demons and idols of gold and silver and bronze and stone and wood, which cannot see or hear or walk, nor did they repent of their murders or their sorceries or their sexual immorality or their thefts" (verses 20–21).

Before the seventh trumpet sounds, two inset chapters explain that John has a commission to prophesy again "about [or, better translated, "against"] many peoples and nations and languages and kings" (Revelation 10:11), and that two human witnesses will come to warn the world of God's coming final intervention (Revelation 11:3–12). John's message comes symbolically in the form of a scroll he must eat, which is both bitter and sweet. Like the prophet Ezekiel who had a similar experience with God's word (see Ezekiel 2:8–3:3), John tastes the message as sweet. But it is bitter in his stomach because of the bad news it brings for humanity.

The two witnesses, who prophesy in the city of Jerusalem for three and a half years, also bring a message of warning that goes unheeded until after they are killed for their efforts and resurrected. Only then do some repent (Revelation 11:13)—the only incidence in the entire book of people turning to God as a result of punitive judgment. This is all preparatory to the third woe and the sounding of the seventh trumpet when loud voices in heaven announce, "The kingdom of the world has become the kingdom of our Lord and of his Christ, and he shall reign forever and ever" (verse 15).

Essential Background

At this point John's attention is turned to several informative scenes—further insets in the story flow that appear to delay the action but in fact set up the denouement that is coming in human history. What John is asked to write down is nothing less than the explanation of why the world has been so opposed to God and His servants, why with few exceptions it will not repent of its ways, and why the day of God's wrath has to come before there can be peace on earth.

Chapter 12 contains a history of God's people, first as the children of Israel, specifically the tribe of Judah among whom Christ first came, and then as the New Covenant Church persecuted through time. The symbol for the congregation of Israel and the Church is a woman, "clothed with the sun, with the moon under her feet, and on her head a crown of twelve stars" (Revelation 12:1), whose son (Christ) is killed and who must take refuge in the wilderness under God's protection (verse 6) until He returns.

The same chapter describes war in heaven between Satan and his angels and the forces of God. Satan is defeated and thrown back to the earth. Frustrated in his attempt to destroy the woman who is under God's protection, he goes to make war on "the rest of her offspring, on those who keep the commandments of God and hold to the testimony of Jesus" (verse 17; Revelation 13:1). John confirms the beast as a Satanic power: "The beast that I saw was like a leopard; its feet were like a bear's, and its mouth was like a lion's mouth. And to it the dragon gave his power and his throne and great authority" (Revelation 13:2).

What follows is a description of the final manifestation of a politico-religious system that has plagued humanity through the ages, especially the people of God. The prophet Daniel explained to Nebuchadnezzar, king of Babylon, that such a system would persist across four empires, from his reign until the end of this age of man (see Daniel 2 and 7). John happened to be living in the days of the fourth major manifestation—the Roman Empire. What he saw in vision was the same system at the end of this age, after it has morphed and renewed itself several times through the centuries. Consistent with the prophecy in Daniel concerning the eclipsing of human forms of government (Daniel 7:13–14 and 2:44–45), John describes the ultimate globalized politico-religious version of the system and its downfall (Revelation 17 and 18). The long history of this world order will be explored in detail under the forthcoming *Vision Collections* title, *Messiahs! Rulers and the Role of Religion.*

A further inset in the narrative concerns the 144,000 of chapter 7. Having been sealed for protection, here they are pictured, as previously noted, victorious with the returned Christ on Mount Zion (14:1–5). The inset section continues with the appearance of three angels with three messages (verses 6–11). First is a proclamation of good news to all on earth that the final hour has come. God is about to judge. Second, a statement that the great false system, now identified as "Babylon the Great," has fallen. Third, a final warning that the punishment of those in league with the system is imminent. Accordingly, the next inset shows the harvesting of the wicked of the earth for the day of God's intervention.

The Seventh Trumpet

Chapter 15 returns to the story flow with the sounding of the seventh trumpet. This initiates the pouring out of the seven last plagues contained in seven bowls (verses 1–5).

A detailed description of these terrible punishments meted out by angels follows in chapter 16. Those who have aligned themselves with the beast's rule are afflicted with "harmful and painful sores." The second angel's bowl is poured out into the sea and its life forms die. The third angel avenges the blood of the saints by pouring out his bowl on fresh water; it becomes as blood. People are scorched by the sun's heat and curse God for the fourth plague, but they will not repent. The fifth angel targets the throne of the beast, plunging it into darkness, pain and anguish. They, too, do not change their ways.

In the region of the River Euphrates, three unclean spirits are loosed as the sixth bowl is poured out. They are demonic beings who stir up world leaders to assemble at Armageddon and go out to fight the returning Christ. The seventh bowl produces a great earthquake that shakes the world's cities, mountains and islands. Huge hailstones fall, and people once more curse God.

The Great Prostitute

John has alluded to the religious aspects of political order in chapter 13, when he introduced a lamb-dragon figure that promotes worship of the governmental beast and obedience to its economic commands (Revelation 13:11–18). This false prophet represents a false religious system, symbolized by a great whore in the inset chapter 17. The whore in turn rides the political beast, being transported by it but guiding its way.

Chapter 18 describes the effect of Babylon's sudden downfall. The whole world has traded its goods and been dependent on it, acting immorally to gain her favor. But God's people are to have separated themselves from it. They will be saved at the time of Babylon's fall.

The Rule of Christ

The people of God will then participate in the marriage celebration of Christ and His Church, pictured here as bridegroom and bride (Revelation 19:6–9). The inauguration of the kingdom of God, which will span an initial 1,000 years on earth, will coincide with the return of the true Christ as a rider on a white horse (verses 11–16).

The archenemy of humanity will now be restrained: "Then I saw an angel coming down from heaven, holding in his hand the key to the bottomless pit and a great chain. And he seized the dragon, that ancient serpent, who is the devil and Satan, and bound him for a thousand years . . . so that he might not deceive the nations any longer" (Revelation 20:1–3).

The people of God will then join Christ in ruling on the earth. Only after a thousand years will all others come back to life (verse 5). At the close of the millennial period, Satan will be released for a short period. He will again deceive some of the nations and then suffer defeat and eternal punishment (verse 10).

Once Satan is banished, a period of time will be allotted to all who have ever lived and not known and followed God's way, to make the choice to do so (verses 11–13). If they do, they will be given eternal life. If they choose not to participate, which would mean living contrary to the laws that guarantee happiness, God will mercifully end their existence. In the symbolism of the book of Revelation, a lake of fire consumes all who refuse to follow God. This is known as the second death, from which there is no return.

The New Heavens and the New Earth

The last two chapters in Revelation speak about the time beyond the millennial rule of Christ. Though the book has dealt primarily with the end of the age of humanly devised rule, it now turns to the beginning of a limitless future. This is the time when God the Father will take up residence with His people on the earth. The New Jerusalem, a symbol of God's throne, will descend to the earth (Revelation 21:1-3). It will be a time when the problems of this present world will be gone forever: "He will wipe away every tear from their eyes, and death shall be no more, neither shall there be mourning, nor crying, nor pain anymore, for the former things have passed away" (verse 4).

John confirms that the people of God are those who voluntarily choose His way and conquer their own nature and take on God's character (verse 7). But those who do not, suffer great loss: "But as for the cowardly, the faithless, the detestable, as for murderers, the sexually immoral, sorcerers, idolaters, and all liars, their portion will be in the lake that burns with fire and sulfur, which is the second death" (verse 8).

Finally, John is shown the river of the water of life that sustains the tree of life, whose leaves bring healing to all. Night and day are no more, and everyone will see God and live in His light (Revelation 22:1–5).

John's Testimony

John completes the record of all that he saw and heard with Christ's assurance, "I, Jesus, have sent my angel to testify to you about these things for the churches. I am the root and the descendant of David, the bright morning star" (verse 16). He also quotes Christ's threefold promise that He is coming soon (verses 7, 12 and 20).

John's own final comment is a warning to preserve the content of the book, to neither add to nor subtract from it: "I warn everyone who hears the words of the prophecy of this book: if anyone adds to them, God will add to him the plagues described in this book, and if anyone takes away from the words of the book of this prophecy, God will take away his share in the tree of life and in the holy city, which are described in this book" (verses 18–19).

So ends the last letter of the last surviving first-century apostle of Jesus Christ. As noted earlier, nothing definitive is known about when or how John died, but based on several early traditions it likely occurred around the end of the first century, possibly in Ephesus.

Few written records of the Church survive from the decades preceding and following John's death, as though a fog enshrouded that period of church history. What is clear, however, is that the church that reappeared, calling itself Christian, was hardly recognizable as the church Christ had founded. It seems that despite the warnings issued by each of the first-century apostles, Gnostics and other false teachers gained an increasing foothold, so that followers of the Way eventually found themselves marginalized and vastly outnumbered.

Epilogue
There can be no doubt that these first followers held to a common belief and practice.

To the very end of John's writings, his message remained constant: hold fast till the end, and live according to the way of life that Jesus Christ taught and practiced, never losing sight of His promised return and the establishment of a better world.

Like John, each of the other New Testament authors we've considered made important closing comments in their writings. They show consistency of hope, purpose, intent and way of life. There can be no doubt that these first followers held to a common belief and practice. Their assessment of society around was realistic, and their focus was on living in light of the future. The following concluding thoughts provide an appropriate close to this study of their lives and point the way forward for any who would not just listen but also walk in their footsteps.

James tells fellow believers to "be patient . . . until the coming of the Lord. See how the farmer waits for the precious fruit of the earth, being patient about it, until it receives the early and the late rains. You also, be patient. Establish your hearts, for the coming of the Lord is at hand" (James 5:7–8).

Jude contrasts the way of the world around with the way of life the believer must live, and advises: "You, beloved, building yourselves up in your most holy faith and praying in the Holy Spirit, keep yourselves in the love of God, waiting for the mercy of our Lord Jesus Christ that leads to eternal life" (Jude 20–21).

Paul, writing a last letter to his helper Timothy, speaks the timeless truth that "all Scripture is breathed out by God and profitable for teaching, for reproof, for correction, and for training in righteousness, that the man of God may be competent, equipped for every good work" (2 Timothy 3:16–17).

And Peter, having shown the certainty of the coming kingdom of God, instructs, "You therefore, beloved, knowing this beforehand, take care that you are not carried away with the error of lawless people and lose your own stability. But grow in the grace and knowledge of our Lord and Savior Jesus Christ. To him be the glory both now and to the day of eternity. Amen" (2 Peter 3:17–18).